Philosophy-Screens

SUNY series in Contemporary Continental Philosophy

Dennis J. Schmidt, editor

Philosophy-Screens
From Cinema to the Digital Revolution

Mauro Carbone

Translated by
Marta Nijhuis

Published by State University of New York Press, Albany

Philosophie-écrans. Du cinéma à la révolution numérique
© Librairie Philosophique J. VRIN, Paris, 2016.
http://www.vrin.fr

© 2019 State University of New York

All rights reserved

No part of this book may be used or reproduced in any manner whatsoever without written permission. No part of this book may be stored in a retrieval system or transmitted in any form or by any means including electronic, electrostatic, magnetic tape, mechanical, photocopying, recording, or otherwise without the prior permission in writing of the publisher.

For information, contact State University of New York Press, Albany, NY
www.sunypress.edu

Library of Congress Cataloging-in-Publication Data

Names: Carbone, Mauro, 1956– author. | Nijhuis, Marta, 1983– translator.
Title: Philosophy-screens : from cinema to the digital revolution / Mauro Carbone ; translated by Marta Nijhuis.
Other titles: Philosophie-écrans. English
Description: Albany : State University of New York Press, [2019] | Series: SUNY series in contemporary continental philosophy | Includes bibliographical references and index.
Identifiers: LCCN 2018033266 | ISBN 9781438474656 (hardcover : alk. paper) | ISBN 9781438474649 (pbk. : alk. paper) | ISBN 9781438474663 (ebook)
Subjects: LCSH: Motion pictures—Philosophy. | Philosophy, Modern—20th century.
Classification: LCC PN1995 .C341313 2019 | DDC 791.4301—dc23
LC record available at https://lccn.loc.gov/2018033266

10 9 8 7 6 5 4 3 2 1

Contents

List of Illustrations — vii

Preface: In The Light of Our Screens — ix

Acknowledgments — xi

Part One
What Is a "Philosophy-Cinema?"

Chapter One
Sartre and Deleuze via Bergson — 3

Chapter Two
The Philosopher and the Moviemaker: Merleau-Ponty and the
Meaning of Cinema — 9

Chapter Three
The Torn Curtain: Lyotard, the Screen, and a Cinema
Named Desire — 55

Part Two
The Animated Life of Screens

Chapter Four
Delimiting to Exceed: The Theme of the "Arche-Screen"
Founding Itself with Its Variants — 57

Chapter Five
Come Live with Me: The Seduction of the Screens Today   81

Chapter Six
Making Philosophy among and through the Screens   97

Notes   111

Index   147

Illustrations

Figure 2.1 Jean-Luc Godard, *Masculin féminin*, 1966. Film still. © Argos Films.   20

Figure 2.2 Jean Vigo, *Zéro de conduit*, 1933. Film still. © Argos Films. Accessed June 14, 2018. https://archive.org/details/zero_de_conduite.   26

Figure 4.1 Albrecht Dürer, *Draughtsman Making a Perspective Drawing of a Reclining Woman*, 1538. Image courtesy of the Metropolitan Museum of Art, NY. Accessed June 14, 2018. https://www.metmuseum.org/art/collection/search/366555.   59

Figure 4.2 Rembrandt van Rijn, *The Philosopher in Meditation*, 1632. Musée du Louvre, Paris. Image courtesy of Wikimedia Commons. Accessed June 14, 2018. https://commons.wikimedia.org/wiki/File:Rembrandt_-_The_Philosopher_in_Meditation.jpg.   60

Figure 5.1 Edwin S. Porter, *Uncle Josh at the Moving Picture Show*, 1902. Film still. Library of Congress. Accessed June 14, 2018. https://www.loc.gov/item/00694324.   82

Figure 5.2 The crowd at Times Square sees itself on Forever 21's interactive billboard, New York, 2010. Video still. © Digital Billboard by space150/Forever 21. Accessed June 14, 2018. https://vimeo.com/32114343.   87

Figure 5.3 Buster Keaton, *Sherlock Jr.*, 1924. Film still. Accessed June 14, 2018. https://www.youtube.com/watch?v=JRXkAhMYKEc.   88

Figure 5.4　BITcrash44, "how to hack video screens on times square," YouTube, 2011. Video still. Accessed June 14, 2018. https://www.youtube.com/watch?v=s_HUYi9aVvI.　93

Figure 5.5　Mathieu Wothke, *La Piège des Images*, W Atjust, 2011. Video still. Accessed June 14, 2018. https://www.youtube.com/watch?v=rqbVyqkbaDc.　95

Preface

In The Light of our Screens

There is no need to recall the Allegory of the Cave: philosophy always made its distaste for screens quite clear, regardless of the kind. One could even claim that philosophy traditionally identified itself—i.e., *found its very identity*—in a *fight* against the screens, which it assimilated with the illusion, the deceit, the obstacle preventing from the contemplation of truth. Indeed, it is precisely under this sign that philosophy's relation to the cinema began. In 1907, nearly twelve years after the birth of the cinematograph, Henri Bergson stated, in *Creative Evolution*, that this technology rendered but a pure illusion of movement.

Still, if only one looks deeper, things are not quite as simple. Rather, they are ambiguous—even *literally* ambiguous, that is to say, such as to present two possible meanings. In fact, what Plato describes in the Allegory of the Cave is not a single screen, but precisely *two*: one showing, the other one concealing; both converging, however, in their global effect, as the *two complementary possibilities of one single configuration*. In the following pages, I shall call such a configuration the *arche-screen*.

The ambiguity of this configuration makes us understand that philosophy's relations to the screens have, in turn, always been ambiguous. Actually, as I suggested before, on the one hand, philosophy has always accused the screens of *not making us see* what it is decisive to know. Still, on the other hand, philosophy invariably ended up looking for some sort of screen, precisely to *make us see*, through them, at least the *image* of what it wants us to know. The Bergsonian condemnation of the cinematograph may just as well exemplify the first side of such an ambiguous relationship, while the metaphor of the "black screen" that

Bergson himself posits in Matter and Memory, as well as the attempts of twentieth-century French philosophy to rehabilitate the cinema and its screen—which I will take into account in the initial part of the book—rather refer to the other side. Indeed, this latter side suggests that (and why) philosophy has always had—generally in an implicit and (too) often unavowed way—its own specific *need for screens*. The reasons for such an exigency do not seem too different from the ones concerning our very vision, which is itself marked by a constitutive screens necessity, since it is the visual perception of a figure on a ground, that is to say, precisely a screen.

However, what happens when considering that the screens have a long and diverse cultural history? What happens when considering that such a history has been sedimenting in that of the very term defining them and of others that have gradually matched it in order to specify the function that the screens would provide? What happens when considering that such a history has also been sedimenting in certain metaphors through which we have tried to *find figures* that could give a fundament to our ways to conceive the screens themselves? And moreover, what happens when considering that those screens, as announced in the title of this book's second part, keep living "an animated life," namely, a life that animates ours all the more? Eventually, what happens when considering that our screens experience has crossed deep mutations and does not cease to report new ones, which cannot but influence and hence modify our ways of perceiving, desiring, knowing, and thinking? Such are questions that the philosophical reflection can no longer elude, not only as they strongly demand to be interrogated, but also as they interrogate it in turn. Let us hence go back to the beginning: What happens if the mutations that I just recalled no longer allow to continue to expect that philosophy identifies itself with the "fight against the screens"? Gilles Deleuze had raised a similar question when referring to the inescapable novelty of the advent of the cinema, which consequently demanded the elaboration of what he once called "a philosophy-cinema." The choice to echo, in the title of this book, such an amazing formulation—unexplored by Deleuze himself in the first place—aims at reviving the radicalness of the need it expresses, by trying to qualify, detail, and see it in a new light—the light of our screens.

Acknowledgments

The starting points for this book are the research cores of my previous works *The Flesh of Images: Merleau-Ponty Between Painting and Cinema* (2015, originally published in French in 2011) and *Être morts ensemble: l'événement du 11 septembre 2001* (2013), whose last chapter I have developed and updated in the article "Falling Man: The Time of Trauma, the Time of (Certain) Images."[1]

I had the chance to develop and enhance such research cores thanks to the extraordinary opportunity I was given by being appointed Senior Member of the *Institut Universitaire de France*, which was crucial in providing me with the conditions to continue my researches. In fact, membership in such a prestigious French institution allowed me to establish and consolidate scientific contacts that were decisively beneficial to the preparation of the present book. My warmest thanks are hence addressed, first of all, to the *Institut Universitaire de France* as well as to the colleagues who supported my candidacy, namely, Renaud Barbaras and Vivian Sobchack. Also, I would like to thank from the bottom of my heart, for a continuous and friendly exchange that was both public and private, Emmanuel Alloa, Gabriela Basterra, Giovanna Borradori, Francesco Casetti, Michele Cometa, Jean-Pierre Esquenazi, Vittorio Gallese, Richard Grusin, Galen Johnson, W. J. T. Mitchell, Pietro Montani, Andrea Pinotti, Pierre Rodrigo, Emmanuel de Saint Aubert, Antonio Somaini, Bernard Stiegler, Luc Vancheri. For including me in the precious discussions that allowed me to submit the reflections I was elaborating for this book to the remarks of students and specialists from very different nations and domains, I am extremely grateful to Arthur Cools, Roberto De Gaetano, Élie During, Ericson Falabretti, Arild Fetveit, Amy Foley, Jean-Baptiste Joinet, Rajiv Kaushik, José Manuel Martins,

Marcos José Müller, Peter Reynaert, Jim Risser, Alejandro Vallega, Daniela Vallega-Neu. In turn, Dudley Andrew, Tom Gunning, Masaki Kondo, and Erica Nijhuis, by virtue of their competences and insight, gave me very important suggestions, confirmations, and critical remarks for which I am truly thankful.

I would like to address special thanks to the group of young scholars who completed their studies under my supervision and with whom, over the past few years in Lyon, I have shared many projects and achievements—both individual and collective—in a most enriching atmosphere from a human as well as from a scientific point of view: Jacopo Bodini, Francesco Caddeo, Stanislas de Courville, Anna Caterina Dalmasso, Lucia Lo Marco, Marta Nijhuis. With some of them, I had the pleasure and privilege to engage in a common research, whose most different theoretical and logistic aspects we have been approaching on a daily basis over the years. To their cleverness, passion, culture, and sensitivity this book owes a lot. Moreover, this book owes to Marta Nijhuis the commitment and rigor she accepted to provide it with her always attentive, patient, and insightful care, so as to realize the present English version on time, despite her burdensome personal and professional engagements. For the enthusiasm by which they welcomed the proposal to publish such English version, I am deeply grateful to the director of the present collection, Dennis Schmidt, and to Andrew Kenyon, Philosophy Acquisitions Editor at SUNY Press. Besides, since a first version of certain pages from this book had already appeared in a number of journals and collective works, I take this opportunity to also thank their editors and publishing houses.

The moment of concluding a book inevitably being a time for making an assessment, it is also a time for expressing my gratitude to the colleagues of the Philosophy Faculty of the Université Jean Moulin Lyon 3 for the way in which they made me feel welcome, as well as to my own university for its support throughout my research projects. A proposal concerning precisely the topics discussed in the present study was even awarded extraordinary support.

This book is dedicated to someone who has long been persuaded he had given up once and for all his passion for cinema in favor of his love for philosophy. Luckily, he was wrong.

Part One

What Is a "Philosophy-Cinema?"

> I wasn't stupid enough to want to create a philosophy of cinema.
> —Gilles Deleuze, "The Brain Is the Screen"

1

Sartre and Deleuze via Bergson

Sartre Anticipates Deleuze:
The Cinema, a "Bergsonian Art"

"Together we would like to be the Humpty-Dumpty of philosophy, or its Laurel and Hardy. A philosophy-cinema."[1] Thus writes Deleuze, referring to himself and to Félix Guattari, in his "Note to the Italian Edition of *The Logic of Sense*," published in 1974. This sentence seems to echo the passage by which, six years earlier, he had finished the Preface to *Difference and Repetition*: "The time is coming when it will hardly be possible to write a book of philosophy as it has been done for so long: 'Ah! The old style . . .' The search for a new means of philosophical expression was begun by Nietzsche and must be pursued today in relation to the renewal of certain other arts, such as the theatre or the cinema."[2] In short, Deleuze found that the novelty of cinema implied a renewal of the philosophical questions concerning not only our relationships to ourselves, to the others, to the things, and to the world, but also—and inevitably—concerning philosophy itself: that is, concerning its expressive style and, hence, the very style of its own thinking. Indeed, the question of the "philosophy-cinema" does not belong to a single thinker. Rather, it involves a whole *epoch*, as the Preface to *Difference and Repetition* suggested. In this sense, it is a question regarding thinking itself. As such—that is to say, precisely as it concerns a whole epoch—it is not surprising to see it emerge, every now and then, all through that epoch. Actually, also Jean-Paul Sartre, in a posthumously published writing, seems to have come across this question—with the imprudence of his (then) twenties. Apparently, such writing dates back to his last *khâgne*[3] trimester (1924) or to his first year at the École Normale Supérieure (1924–25);

in any case, well before his first approach to phenomenology, which was to occur about ten years later. The writing's title is "Apologie pour le cinéma. Défense et illustration d'un Art international [Apology for the Cinema. Defense and Illustration of an International Art]."[4]

The starting point Sartre chose for this writing is what his former philosophy teacher and one of the time's most influential "masters of thinking"—namely, Emile-Auguste Chartier, better known as Alain—maintained in one of his own 1923 *Propos sur l'esthétique* (Thoughts on Aesthetics), significantly titled "L'immobile [Immobility]."

This is how Alain started: "Art expresses human power through immobility. There is no better sign of a soul's strength than immobility, since the thinking is recognizable in it."[5] He concluded by affirming that "the art of the screen provides an *a contrario* evidence"[6] of this artistic research of immobility, "without even looking for it; for the perpetual movement is the very law of films, not only because speech is lacking completely—and it becomes clear that to be mute from birth does not mean to keep silent—but most of all because the actor feels obliged to be restless, as if to pay homage to the mechanical invention."[7]

In short, this is roughly the syllogism proposed by Alain: if all art is a "search of immobility in movement,"[8] and if—as we just read—"the perpetual movement is the very law of films," then "the art of the screen" is not an actual art.

The young Sartre highlights that he traces in Alain's question "the elements [of a problem] that is far more important than the sterile discussions of someone like Winckelmann: does [beauty consist] in immobility or rather in change?"[9] Indeed, for Sartre, the most important problem is raised by the passage in which we heard Alain affirm that *thinking is recognizable in immobility*. In reconsidering this question, Sartre gives it a significant twist. Alain's thesis suggested that thinking is, by its very essence, recognizable in immobility. In Sartre's opinion, such a thesis expresses the attachment (the word he uses is, precisely, *attached* [*attaché*]) of the human mind "to what is motionless, and not only in aesthetics."[10] Sartre hence explains that "[i]t is [easier to understand] the immutable. In particular, it is easier to love what does not change, and one tries to blind one's self to this point: 'You have not changed. You still look the same.'"[11] It is not hard to trace, in this sentence, some underlying Bergsonian echoes—which will later be confirmed—concerning the interpretation of our practical life.

Sartre hence seems to suggest that Platonism understood as the thinking of Being meant as *endurance* consists precisely in this effort to blind one's self. Still, "a new philosophy has dethroned that of the immutable Ideas,"[12] he claims. However, he only names it a few lines farther. "At the moment, there is no reality outside change. Will aesthetics not benefit from this?"[13] Such a question allows Sartre to introduce his reflection on the cinema, for—as he will explain further—the cinema "inaugurates mobility in aesthetics."[14]

It looks as if we could synthesize things as follows: for Sartre, the cinema—by inaugurating mobility in aesthetics—has helped to unveil the fact that the supposed acknowledgment of thinking's essence in what is motionless was but an attachment to what is "easier." Hence, the cinema questions philosophy itself, for it "dethrones" Platonism and literally gets us thinking *anew*. Or rather, what shall be thought anew imposes onto philosophy, no less inevitably, the responsibility to think *of itself* as a "philosophy-cinema," we might say echoing Deleuze.

Yet, there is more. To Alain's dismissive judgment apropos of the cinema's mutism, Sartre responds as follows: "We are closer to non-speaking actors, who do in fact sing, and their song (I mean, that of the violins) signifies much better whatever they may say [. . .] does better than just teaching us what Mary Pickford thinks, since it makes us think as she does."[15]

On this basis, he hence recurs "to some Bergsonian passages,"[16] in which one can notice the repeated reference to the *melody* as an example of composed and yet undecomposable movement. Indeed, it is through these passages by the grand philosopher that the young student aims at "making understand that a film, with its sound accompaniment, is a consciousness like ours."[17] In other words—as in the case of a melody—it is "an indivisible flow."[18] Besides, in the previous lines, Sartre had already declared that, since it "inaugurates mobility in aesthetics," "the cinema provides the formula of a Bergsonian art."[19] Thus, he unveiled the identity of the "new philosophy" to which he was referring, and, by such means, he claimed something that, surprisingly enough, would anticipate in one single shot the double action by which, in 1983, Deleuze would begin, in his turn, the *Movement-Image*.

Indeed, the first chapter of this book by Deleuze appeared to be in accordance with the substance of the Sartrean judgment. At the same time, it implicitly reminded us that Bergson himself would have never allowed such a judgment, for it was he who, in *Creative Evolution* (1907), matched the "typical example of false movement"[20] precisely with the cinema, which had then been born only a dozen years earlier and, still according to Bergson, claimed to reconstruct movement itself as a sum of "immobile sections and abstract time."[21]

The problem is raised, first of all, by the fact that in a movie, as we know, at each second comes a succession of a certain number of photograms—between sixteen and eighteen at the time of silent pictures, later twenty-four. Such photograms are spaced by as many instants of black, which remain unperceived by the spectator. In fact, each of these motionless photograms is separated from the others by such an exiguous temporal gap that the ensemble we perceive creates an impression of continuity.

Sartre seems to refer precisely to this question when, in his "Apologie pour le cinéma," he writes: "You may even consider it [the film] as a roll of motionless negatives; this is no more a film than the water from the tank is the water from the source, or a consciousness divided by associationism is the actual consciousness."[22] Convinced that one may say about the film what Bergson claimed apropos of the melody—and suggesting a little further that their respective indivisibility is one and the same with the *rhythm* that characterizes both[23]—the young Sartre peremptorily stresses that "[t]he essence of the film is in mobility and in duration."[24]

About sixty years later, it is Deleuze who will proceed in a similar direction, by recurring precisely to Bergson so as to criticize the judgment on cinema, which Bergson himself had expressed in *Creative Evolution*: "Cinema does not give us an image to which movement is added, it immediately gives us a movement-image."[25] Deleuze also makes clear that this is the movement-image Bergson himself had discovered—in the first chapter of *Matter and Memory*—as he overcame the opposition between "[m]ovement, as physical reality in the external world, and the image, as psychic reality in consciousness."[26]

Sartre Quits Bergsonianism and Film Theory

However, the parallel between the young Sartre's path and that of Deleuze's book comes to an end here, for they will move on in opposite directions. Starting from 1933, Sartre will discover Husserl's phenomenology, which he finds—with respect to his desire to move "toward concreteness"[27]—more satisfactory than Bergson's thinking. Of course, such concreteness includes that of images.[28] As for Deleuze, he will describe Bergson's and Husserl's paths as two antagonist replies to the same historical need "to overcome this duality of image and movement, of consciousness and thing."[29] As is well known, he will then take sides in favor of Bergson's reply against Husserl's. Hence, if the editors of the young Sartre's "Bergsonian" text considered it as a "pre-phenomenological"[30] writing, Deleuze rather qualifies the position Sartre assumed after the encounter with phenomenology in terms of "anti-Bergsonianism."[31] Of course, at the time Deleuze did not know this text by the young Sartre. Still, Sartre's reference to the first chapter of *Matter and Memory* after his discovery of the Husserlian intentionality implicitly reckons a common aim in Bergson's and Husserl's ways, as well as some at least partially similar approaches.[32] Since Deleuze will do the same in *The Movement-Image*, the polemic label by which he marks Sartre frankly seems a little excessive. In fact, a critical attitude toward the Bergsonian conception of the image is not necessarily considerable as "anti-Bergsonianism."

Besides, only a few pages before this claim, Deleuze had already highlighted that, when "making an inventory and analysis of all kinds of images in *The Imagination*," Sartre the phenomenologist "does not cite the cinematographic image."[33] Why such silence? Evidently, all attempts to answer this question can only be hypothetical. Nevertheless, it has to be observed that, by such silence, Sartre at least ends up avoiding the temptation of tracing everything back to the philosophical current that, by then, had become his main reference. This is something it is important to highlight, I believe. For indeed, both in the young Sartre of the "Apologie pour le cinema" and in the Deleuze of *Difference and Repetition*, we found a suggestion to consider the cinema as a symptom of an epoch's novelty; a novelty that, beginning with aesthetics, ends up implying ontology, and even philosophy as a whole. Actually, we have heard the two philosophers manifest the intention of approaching the cinema not so much in order to envelop it in a previously elaborated thinking, but rather in order to find at work in it a type of thinking that philosophy as such *is not yet able to think of*. Still, we have seen the young Sartre as well as the Deleuze of the cinema diptych[34] characterize the cinema as a "Bergsonian art." In short, we have seen them share the tendency to interpret the cinema by opposing to the insufficiencies of the philosophical tradition the novelties of their own reference philosophy, which they would make become a sort of "philosophy-cinema."[35] Is this not a little too easy, though? If one looks deeper, the fact that, after the discovery of phenomenology, Sartre avoids assuming or hesitates to assume once more his previous attitude seems to authorize us to eventually think that a "philosophy-cinema" still basically remains *to be done*.

Indeed, if it is true—as Alain seems to claim and the young Sartre is willing to believe—that mobility has been introduced in art only thanks to the cinema; if, moreover, as Deleuze maintains, the cinema "immediately gives us a movement-image" that disavows the opposition between physical and psychic reality, between exterior and interior, between space and time, between the things and the gaze; then the "philosophy-cinema" deserves to be called not only to think of our new relation toward ourselves, the others, the things, the world—of which the advent of the cinema is, as I said before, a symptom—but also, in the name of that same need and according to such a mutated relationship, to rethink its own style of thinking and expression. In other words, the "philosophy-cinema," rather than being called to think of the cinema by playing once more the role of a "form of reflection applied to a previously given object,"[36] is called to *think* of the Being and itself *according to the cinema*.

2

The Philosopher and the Moviemaker

Merleau-Ponty and the Meaning of Cinema*

Making Seen instead of Explaining: The Historical Convergence of Cinema and Philosophy according to Merleau-Ponty

The elements of logical continuity of the young Sartre's "Bergsonian" text and the exigencies leading him toward phenomenology are evoked by Pascale Fautrier: "The pre-phenomenological (Bergsonian) reflections on consciousness, which can be found in Sartre's *juvenilia* on cinema, and his analogy of the film, understood as a synthetic unity of indecomposable moving images, with consciousness as a continuous activity (rather than a group of psychic facts), had to be confirmed by his discovery of Husserl in 1933."[1] Besides, Fautrier immediately highlights that "[i]t will be Merleau-Ponty's task to formulate, in 1945 (that is, at the same time of his participation in the creation of *Les Temps Modernes*, i.e. the journal directed by Sartre) this congruent contemporaneity between phenomenology's philosophical evolutions and the invention of the cinema."

As we know, the circumstance Pascale Fautrier refers to is the lecture titled "The Film and the New Psychology," which Merleau-Ponty gave on March 13, 1945 at the Institut des Hautes Études Cinématographiques (IDHEC) in Paris, which was then "presided by Marcel L'Herbier and

---

*This chapter enriches and develops in light of present research the one I published under a similar title in Mauro Carbone, *La chair des images: Merleau-Ponty entre peinture et cinéma* (Paris: Vrin, 2011), trans. Marta Nijhuis, *The Flesh of Images: Merleau-Ponty between Painting and Cinema* (Albany: State University of New York Press, 2015), 41–61.

directed by Pierre Gérin."[2] The invitation to give this lecture might have been solicited by André Bazin,[3] namely, the founder-to-be of the *Cahiers du cinéma* and the spiritual father of the *Nouvelle Vague*. Although *Les Temps Modernes* only published in 1947 a text presented as that of Merleau-Ponty's IDHEC lecture,[4] already in October 1945 the French philosopher had accepted to *resume*—such is the term used in the editorial premise—this lecture in the weekly journal *L'écran français*. In his short article, titled "Cinéma et psychologie,"[5] Merleau-Ponty at once emphasizes, makes clear, and synthesizes certain considerations that can be found randomly in a number of his coeval writings. Indeed, he affirms that "[t]here are great classic works taking into account the human being from an outer standpoint, as do the cinema, modern psychology, and the American novel."[6]

Merleau-Ponty hence thinks that such cultural domains try—each in its own way—"to express human beings by their visible behavior," as he writes a little farther on. The same idea returns in his conclusions with, in addition, an epochal nuance: "If cinema, psychology, and literature agree in expressing the human being from an outer standpoint, this is not a whim of fashion, but an exigency of the human condition that classic art itself has not ignored."[7]

A similar, yet stronger, epochal nuance appears in a far more famous Merleau-Pontian coeval passage, which concludes the Preface to *Phenomenology of Perception*, and explains that "[i]f phenomenology was a movement prior to having been a doctrine or a system, this is neither accidental nor a deception. Phenomenology is as painstaking as the works of Balzac, Proust, Valéry, or Cézanne—through the same kind of attention and wonder, the same demand for awareness, the same will to grasp the sense of the world or of history in its nascent state. As such, phenomenology merges with the effort of modern thought."[8]

From a formal point of view, this passage is similar to the aforementioned one; however, as far as its content is concerned, it does not refer to the cinema, nor to psychology. Still, it evokes phenomenology and Cézanne's painting, as well as literature (which, in this particular case, is exclusively French). What it is most important to observe, however, is that, by juxtaposing these passages, one can trace the whole of the cultural domains that are approached in the "Arts" (in French "*Ouvrages*") section of *Sense and Non-Sense*, namely, the 1948 book that gathers the essays published by Merleau-Ponty in the previous years.[9] In fact, in this section, on the one hand, we obviously come across Cézanne's painting, and, on the other, we come across "The Film and the New Psychology," in the homonym essay, whose last part brings along also phenomenology and, more generally, "contemporary philosophy."[10] Moreover, there are two essays focused on Sartre's and Simone de Beauvoir's novels, to wit, respectively, "A Scandalous Author" and "Metaphysics and the Novel." The latter reveals that there is, in literature no less than in the aforementioned domains, an exigency to "make seen." Indeed, in this text Merleau-Ponty claims that, "since the end of the 19th century,"[11] "Philosophical expression assumes the same ambiguities as literary expression, if the world is such that it cannot be expressed except in 'stories' and, as it were, *pointed at*."[12]

Hence, our starting point, namely, the article for *L'écran français*, confirms the idea that, in the immediate second postwar period, Merleau-Ponty's reflection on the arts and literature is not a set of random remarks and contributions, but is based on some strong guidelines providing it with a clear consistency. Among these "guidelines," at least three can be listed: (1) it is possible, in our time, to figure out a convergence between the novel, painting, and the cinema; (2) such a convergence can be extended also to the *Gestalt* psychology and to contemporary philosophy, particularly phenomenology; (3) the core of such a convergence is the focus on the visible, which is explicit, on the one hand, in the topic concerning our relation to the world, and, on the other hand, in that regarding our relation to the others.

Let us now take into account "The Film and the New Psychology," the opening of which is precisely consecrated to the topic of our relation to the world. In this essay, Merleau-Ponty points out that the psychology he characterizes as "classical" tends to attribute a primary role, in our sensible knowledge, to *sensations*, meant as the *punctual* effects of as many local excitements that intelligence and memory would *successively* have the task of composing in a unitary picture. Instead, as Merleau-Ponty highlights, the "new psychology" shows that what should be considered as *primary* is *perception*, understood as the sensible apprehension of a phenomenon as a whole.

On this basis, the "new psychology" points out the *synesthetic* characteristic of perception, in virtue of which perception shall not be considered as "a sum of visual, tactile, and audible givens,"[13] for it "speaks to all my senses at once."[14] More generally, Merleau-Ponty judges that "[b]y resolutely rejecting the notion of sensation," the theory of form (*Gestalttheorie*) "teaches us to stop distinguishing between signs and their significance, between what is sensed and what is judged."[15]

As we already remarked by examining the passages from Merleau-Ponty's short article published in October 1945, also in the case of the topic of our relation to others, the French philosopher considers that the "new psychology" brings along a "new concept" of their *perception*, on the basis of which one shall reject "the distinction between inner observation, or introspection, and outer observation."[16] Indeed, "we must reject that prejudice which makes 'inner realities' out of love, hate or anger, leaving them accessible to one single witness: the person who feels them."[17] In fact, according to Merleau-Ponty, the "new psychology" shows that "[a]nger, shame, hate, and love are not psychic facts hidden at the bottom of another's consciousness: they are types of behavior or styles of conduct which are visible from the outside."[18]

Merleau-Ponty claims that "the best observation of the aestheticians of the cinema"[19] converges with such novelties in psychology. He makes every effort to highlight them by considering "film as a perceptual object,"[20] that is, as explained by Enzo Paci in his introduction to the Italian translation of *Sense and Non-Sense*, by considering "the cinema [. . .] as a moving form (meant as *Gestalt*),"[21] or as "an indivisible flow"—to say it with the terms we found in the young Sartre's writing.

On this subject, Merleau-Ponty specifies that "a film is not a sum total of images, but a temporal *Gestalt*."[22] Within this temporal *Gestalt*, which is essentially characterized by its *rhythm*, "the meaning of a shot therefore depends on what precedes it in the movie, and this succession of scenes creates a new reality which is not merely the sum of its parts."[23] On the basis of such a definition, Merleau-Ponty describes a famous, and yet lost, cinematic sequence that he attributed to Vsevolod Pudovkin, but which had actually been realized by his master Lev Kuleshov, namely the founder, with Dziga Vertov, of the Soviet cinema. In this sequence, Kuleshov meant to account for the creative role of montage, which he considered to be the cinema's main form of expression.

> One day Pudovkin took a close-up of Mosjoukin with a completely impassive expression and projected it after showing: first, a bowl of soup, then, a young woman lying dead in her coffin, and, last, a child playing with a teddy-bear. The first thing noticed was that Mosjoukin seemed to be looking at

the bowl, the young woman, and the child, and next one noted that he was looking pensively at the dish, that he wore an expression of sorrow when looking at the woman, and that he had a glowing smile for the child. The audience was amazed at his variety of expression although the same shot had actually been used all three times and was, if anything, remarkably inexpressive.[24]

In the fine essay in which he comments on Merleau-Ponty's text,[25] Pierre Rodrigo identifies the aforementioned passage as "the heart of the lecture's reasoning,"[26] reporting that the reference to "this *specific* feature of the cinematic art, i.e., montage"[27] opens up within such reasoning "an evident lacuna: nothing is said about the significant power of image *as such*."[28] This is how, according to him, the Merleau-Pontian reasoning reveals image "as the *atom* of meaning with which montage has to be involved—just like the *word* is the atom of meaning in classical linguistics."[29] Because of this, Rodrigo stresses, by absolutizing the teaching of the Soviet silent cinema such reasoning focuses precisely on montage, that is to say on the meaning as it emerges *among* images, just like—within a sentence—it emerges *among* words. Instead, he claims that—when recognized in its expressive complexity, which will be enhanced by sound cinema—"a cinematic image is a sentence, not merely a word."[30]

Sure enough, Rodrigo's claim can be shared fully. However, the reasoning developed by Merleau-Ponty in the IDHEC lecture seems to be supported by many good arguments.

Let us leave aside the fact that the privilege accorded by Soviet silent cinema to montage is no more questionable than the obsession for long takes—recalled by Rodrigo[31]—which André Bazin sets up against it. Still, it remains to be remarked, first of all, that such a privilege appears particularly useful for the goal declared in Merleau-Ponty's lecture, that is, to show that "we can apply what we have just said about perception in general to the perception of a film,"[32] a goal which the lecture itself clearly expresses in the beginning of its second half, shifting the reflection from the "new psychology" to the cinema. Indeed, it is true that this second half does not really limit itself to "applying to the film perception" the psychological principles explained in the first half, and it is true that, on the contrary, by confronting the cinema, it "retrospectively transforms everything which could be said until then."[33] However, it is no less true that the cinematic montage appears as a particularly effective example of that element of novelty introduced by the *Gestaltpsychologie*, referring to which Merleau-Ponty had started his talk: namely, that "groups rather than juxtaposed elements are principal and primary in our perception."[34]

On the other hand, straight after having expressed such a characteristic, he provided not only visual but also auditory examples, focusing them on the example of melody. And we know that this is no less fundamental for Bergson,[35] than it is for the *Gestalttheorie*. As Merleau-Ponty writes, "The melody is not a sum of notes, since each note only counts by virtue of the function it serves in the whole [. . .] Such a perception of the whole is more natural and more primary than the perception of isolated elements."[36]

And the example of melody is precisely the one Merleau-Ponty refers to when he comes to talk about the Kuleshov effect. He in fact introduces it by pointing out that it "clearly shows the *melodic* unity of films,"[37] for he is interested in highlighting that the film, just like a musical melody, is "a temporal *Gestalt*."[38]

Therefore, differently from what Rodrigo's criticism suggests, it seems to me that, while commenting on the Kuleshov effect, Merleau-Ponty does not have in mind the assimilation of the single cinematic image to the verbal atom of a sentence, but rather *to an isolated musical note*. However, considering such a note in this way indeed appears abstract. On the other hand, even the main character of the first volume of Proust's *Recherche*, Swann, understood this issue in the pages Merleau-Ponty recalled in *Phenomenology of Perception*,[39] which was published in the same year in which the lecture at the IDHEC was given. In those pages, Proust wrote:

> When [. . .] he [i.e., Swann] had sought to disentangle from his confused impressions how it was that it [i.e., the little phrase] swept over and enveloped him, he had observed that it was to the closeness of the intervals between the five notes which composed it and to the constant repetition of two of them that was due that impression of a frigid and withdrawn sweetness; but in reality he knew that he was basing this conclusion not upon the phrase itself, but merely upon certain equivalents, substituted (for his mind's convenience) for the mysterious entity of which he had become aware [. . .] when for the first time he had heard the sonata played.[40]

Hence, not differently from Swann, Merleau-Ponty knows that he would never come across what really gives sense to the considered expressive unity—the little musical phrase in one case, the cinematic sequence in the other—if he disassembled its *form* (i.e., *Gestalt*) in order to analyze its single components. In fact, as he explains, "analytical perception, through which we arrive at absolute value of the separate elements, is a belated and rare attitude—that of the scientist who observes or the philosopher who reflects,"[41] as well as, we might add, that of the specialist in aesthetics or film studies. Precisely for this reason, by considering the Kuleshov effect, Merleau-Ponty means to focus on "the perception of forms, understood very broadly as structure, grouping, or configuration [which] should be considered our spontaneous way of perceiving."[42]

Implicitly, Merleau-Ponty then contributes to freeing the cinema from the heavy claim staked by Henri Bergson—I have already made reference to this—with the famous judgment he expressed in the fourth chapter of *Creative Evolution*. Here Bergson had in turn drawn a parallel between our perception and the working of cinema, but in such a way as to disavow the knowledge of becoming that both our perception and the working of cinema claimed to offer us:

> Such is the contrivance of the cinematograph. And such is also that of our knowledge. Instead of attaching ourselves to the inner becoming of things, we place ourselves outside them in order to recompose their becoming artificially. We take snapshots, as it were, of the passing reality, and as these are characteristic of the reality, we have only to string them on a becoming, abstract, uniform and invisible, situated at the back of the apparatus of knowledge, in order to imitate what there is that is characteristic in this becoming itself. Perception, intellection, language, so proceed in general. Whether we would think becoming, or express it, or even perceive it, we hardly do anything else than set going a kind of cinematograph inside us. We may therefore sum up what we have been saying in the conclusion that the *mechanism of our ordinary knowledge is of a cinematographical kind*.[43]

If understood literally, this latter claim could also summarize the meaning of Merleau-Ponty's lecture, in which he indeed affirms that "we can apply what we have just said about perception in general to the perception of a film."⁴⁴ But it is evident that Merleau-Ponty can come to a conclusion so similar to that of Bergson only *by reversing* its premises: our spontaneous perception is not analytic, but synthetic, and *precisely for this reason* it can be considered "cinematic" by nature. In fact, within its synthetic character we find at work dynamics that are essential for providing us with the *unity* of a perceived form as well as that of a cinematic sequence: far from being *artificial*, as Bergson tends to characterize them, they contribute instead to the *truth* of our perceptions.

In the light of this, the reason why Merleau-Ponty's lecture does not focus on "the significative power of image *as such*,"⁴⁵ to recall the terms of Rodrigo's criticism, may be better understood. Indeed, to focus on such power would be to miss that *specificity* of the cinematic expression that does not consist so much in montage—which, instead, is a consequence of this specificity—but rather in its characteristic of "temporal *Gestalt*." Also by means of this remark on the Kuleshov effect, Merleau-Ponty's aim is such specificity: this is why he avoids focusing on "image as such," for precisely focusing on it would make it become that "atomic" element Rodrigo blames him for reducing the image to.

Instead, the characterization of film assumed by Merleau-Ponty, far from making him lose his attention to images, leads him to highlight how much "the time-factor for each shot"⁴⁶ means to the film itself, to remind us that "the alternation of words and silence is manipulated to create the most effective image,"⁴⁷ to focus, in a word, on the "internal rhythm of the scene," as we may say, recalling the phrase used by Maurice Jaubert.⁴⁸

Indeed, according to such a characterization of film, as Jean-Pierre Charcosset explains,

> the perception of an image [. . .] itself depends upon the perception of the sequence in which it is integrated. So far that the same shot is perceived in a different way depending on the shots that precede it and on those that follow it. But such a *Gestalt* is temporal not only insofar as its projection "requires time," but most of all insofar as the sense of a shot varies depending on its duration. From this, a first consequence can be drawn: the sense of a film depends less on the images of which it is composed than on the *rhythm* of its images.⁴⁹

Such a consequence implies another one, which consists in revealing the fictional characteristics underlying the film's apparent realism. "[W]hat supports this ambiguity is the fact that movies do have a basic realism," Merleau-Ponty remarks. "That does not mean, however, that the movies are fated to let us see and hear what we would see and hear if we were present at the events being related."[50] Both the fictional characteristic and the apparent realism of the film are read according to a perspective explicitly referring to Kant's aesthetics. In particular, the reference concerns the definition of "aesthetic ideas" formulated in §49 of the *Critique of the Power of Judgment*. Elaborated by the artist's or writer's imagination and embodied in the beauty of the work they created, aesthetic ideas occasion "much thinking,"[51] without being completely conceptualizable and conceptually expressible. In the case of cinema, according to Merleau-Ponty's interpretation, this means that the sense "of a film is incorporated to its rhythm just as the meaning of a gesture may immediately be read in that gesture: the film doesn't mean anything but itself. The idea is presented in a nascent state,"[52] that is to say, in its conceptless form. As a consequence, the idea turns out being indiscernible from its sensible[53] manifestation: "[It] emerges from the temporal structure of the film as it does from the coexistence of the parts of a painting [. . .] [A] movie has meaning in the same way that a thing does: neither of them speaks to an isolated understanding: rather, both appeal to our power tacitly to decipher the world or men and to coexist with them."[54]

Here reemerges Merleau-Ponty's conviction concerning the intimate convergence between the "new psychology" and certain artistic and philosophical tendencies of the same epoch. Their mutual intention seems to be that of *teaching us to see the world anew*, as we may say following the famous statement by which Husserl defined the fundamental phenomenological task, and which Merleau-Ponty echoed precisely to describe the aim of the "new psychology": "It re-educates us in how to see the world which we touch at every point of our being."[55] Farther on, the echo of the Husserlian statement returns in terms that can significantly be referred to Proust's literary experience or to Paul Klee's pictorial experience. In fact, in the first volume of the *Recherche*, Proust wrote apropos of the "little phrase" of Vinteuil's sonata: "Those graces of an intimate sorrow, 'twas them that the phrase endeavoured to imitate, to create anew; and even their essence, for all that it consists in being incommunicable and in appearing trivial to everyone save him who has experience of them, the little phrase had captured, had *rendered visible*."⁵⁶ It is well known that it is by a similar expression that Klee opened his *Creative Credo*: "Art does not reproduce the visible; rather, it *makes visible*."⁵⁷ For his part, Merleau-Ponty moves toward the conclusion of his lecture on "The Film and the New Psychology" by suggesting that "[p]henomenological or existential philosophy is largely an expression of surprise at this inherence to the self in the world and in others, a description of this paradox and permeation, and an attempt to make us *see* the bond between subject and world, between subject and others, rather than to *explain* it as the classical philosophies did by resorting to absolute spirit."⁵⁸

We have already mentioned the fact that Merleau-Ponty's lecture is divided into two parts: one is devoted to the new psychology, the other to the cinema, and each is typographically discerned. Another typographical separation flags the end of the second half and heralds its conclusions. It is precisely in the conclusions the aforementioned sentence appears. Here, two conceptual characters that had until then shared the scene are joined by a third one, which had previously occupied a spectator's position, namely, philosophy. Or, more precisely, the "contemporary philosophies,"⁵⁹ whose inspiration is there described as in spontaneous and yet specific accordance with those of the "new psychology" and of cinema. Therefore, by contrast, Bergson's philosophy is implicitly evoked. In fact, even if it is never mentioned during the lecture, it is precisely such philosophy that seems to have suggested to Merleau-Ponty the very choice, at first peculiar, of presenting the acquisitions of "modern psychology"⁶⁰ to an audience of moviemakers-to-be,⁶¹ so as to get to confute in front of them the dismissive Bergsonian judgment on cinema.

Instead, here is "contemporary philosophy"—Merleau-Ponty now declines the name in the singular form—that recognizes itself in motivations, interests, and styles of research in agreement with those of cinema, for indeed—as he explains—contemporary philosophy "consists not in stringing concepts together but in describing the mingling of consciousness with the world, its involvement in a body, and its coexistence with others; and [. . .] this is movie material *par excellence*."⁶²

Retrospectively reasoning, in 1968 the French semiologist and film historian Christian Metz will remark:

Following Merleau-Ponty's lecture on "Le cinéma et la nouvelle psychologie," film began to be defined here and there, or at least approached, from what one called the "phenomenological" angle: a sequence of film, like a spectacle from life, carries its meaning within itself. The signifier is not easily distinguished from the significate. This is an entirely new concept of ordering. The cinema is the "phenomenological" art *par excellence*, the signifier is coextensive with the whole of the significate, the spectacle its own signification, thus short-circuiting the sign itself.[63]

Metz then composes a long list of those who were influenced by such a conception:

This is what was said, in substance, by Souriau, Soriano, Blanchard, Marcel, Cohen-Séat, Bazin, Martin, Ayfre, Astre, Cauliez, Dort, Vailland, Marion, Robbe-Grillet, B. and R. Zazzo and many others [. . .] It is possible, even probable, that they went too far in this direction: for the cinema is after all not life; it is a created spectacle. But let us put these reservations aside for the moment, and simply record what was in fact a convergence in the historical evolution of ideas about film.[64]

It is not difficult to recognize in the perspective that Metz finds drawn by Merleau-Ponty's lecture some of the features that, with greater evidence, had meanwhile come to typify the *Nouvelle Vague* cinema. Therefore, it is not surprising to find in a film by its most emblematic *auteur* a quotation of the sentence by which Merleau-Ponty, coming to the conclusions of his lecture, already identified that "convergence" we heard Metz echo almost twenty years later: "The philosopher and the moviemaker share a certain way of being, a certain view of the world which belongs to a generation."[65]

The film in which this sentence appears is *Masculin féminin*;[66] its author, as everyone knows, is Jean-Luc Godard, and it was distributed in 1966. In that same year Robert Bresson's *Au hasard, Balthazar* was also released in France and, in issue 177 of the *Cahiers du cinéma*, a text titled "Le testament de Balthazar" was published. It appeared to be composed of "collected statements" ["*propos recuillis*"] written by Godard

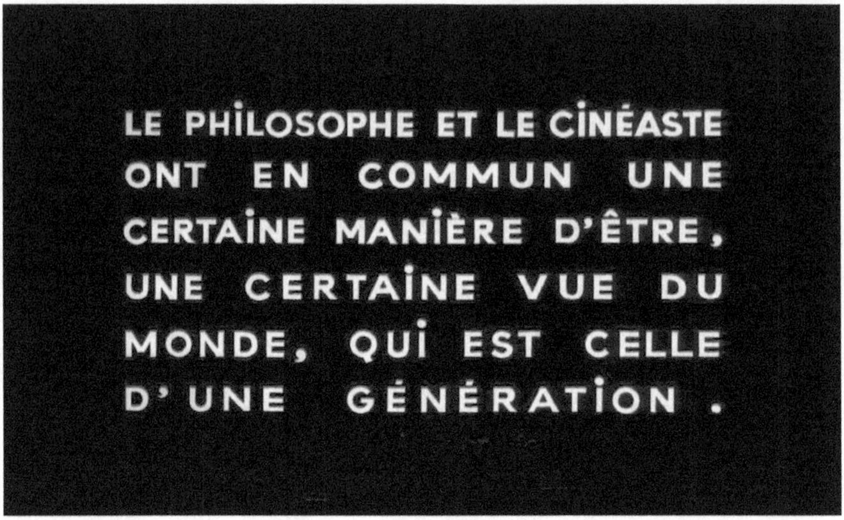

> LE PHILOSOPHE ET LE CINÉASTE ONT EN COMMUN UNE CERTAINE MANIÈRE D'ÊTRE, UNE CERTAINE VUE DU MONDE, QUI EST CELLE D'UNE GÉNÉRATION.

Figure 2.1. Jean-Luc Godard, *Masculin féminin*, 1966. Film still. © Argos Films.

himself along with Merleau-Ponty:[67] to the innocent donkey, protagonist of Bresson's film, are attributed reflections on time, otherness, death, cogito, and freedom. In some of them it is easy to recognize passages taken from the *Phenomenology of Perception*, which, as we know, is coeval with the IDHEC lecture. When he appeared as signee of "Le testament de Balthazar," Merleau-Ponty had been dead for five years.

"The Question of Movement in Cinema"

But let us go back to Merleau-Ponty's sentence concerning the generational convergence of the philosopher and the moviemaker that will excite Godard's enthusiasm, and let us try to trace its developments within Merleau-Ponty's further reflection.

Only fifteen years after Merleau-Ponty wrote this sentence, such a prudent and, to be frank, narrow generational hypothesis will end up being modified in an ontological sense. We see Merleau-Ponty go in such a direction in the preparatory notes for the course titled "Cartesian Ontology and the Ontology of Today," which remained unfinished due to the philosopher's sudden death. These notes present the course, highlighting that the subject after which it is titled "[i]s not the history of philosophy in the current sense: i.e., what has been thought; rather, it is: what has been thought in the context and the horizon of what one thinks—Evoked in order to understand what one thinks. Aim: Contemporary ontology—Starting from this, then toward Descartes and Cartesians, and back to what philosophy can be today."[68]

Actually, this course aims at helping to give a philosophical formulation to the contemporary ontology that Merleau-Ponty characterizes as "a spontaneous philosophy, [a] fundamental thinking."[69] Indeed, according to him such an ontology has so far found its means of expression "especially in literature,"[70] but also in the arts, as he specifies by mentioning in parenthesis, the couple "(painting-cinema)."[71] A few lines farther he adds: "André Bazin ontology of cinema [*André Bazin ontologie du cinéma*]";[72] and once more, a little farther on: "In the arts/ Cinema ontology of cinema—example the question of movement in cinema [*Dans les arts/ Cinéma ontologie du cinéma—Ex. la question du mouvement au cinéma*]."[73]

These course notes hence promised to pick out, in the experiences and the reflections developed by the cinema, some trend lines converging with those sketched by coeval painting and literature in tracing the outline of the "new ontology," which Merleau-Ponty planned "to try to formulate philosophically"[74] precisely with this course. As we read, it was his particular intention to point out such trend lines by way of assuming "the question of movement in cinema" as *exemplum*. It is no surprise, then—but appears all the more interesting—that the only two further traces of the later Merleau-Ponty's reflections on the cinema concern precisely such a question.

One of these traces can be found in a chapter of *The Visible and the Invisible*, which Merleau-Ponty himself will replace with a different version, and which thus appears as an "appendix" in the posthumous volume edited by Claude Lefort. The trace I am alluding to is made of a few intricate lines, in the first part of which the reasons for the Bergsonian condemnation of the cinema seem to be echoed critically: "The discontinuous images of the cinema prove nothing with regard to the phenomenal truth of the movement that connects them before the eyes of the spectator—moreover, they do not even prove that the life world involves movements without a moving object: the moving object could well be projected by him who perceives."[75]

The other trace of the later Merleau-Pontian reflections on cinema lies within the comparison between the various artistic expressions of movement he develops in *Eye and Mind*. Here he writes that "Marey's photographs, the cubists' analysis, Duchamp's *La Mariée* do not move; they give a Zenonian reverie on movement. We see a rigid body as if it were a piece of armor going through its motions; it is here and it is there, magically, but it does not *go* from here to there. Cinema portrays movement, but *how*? It is, as we are inclined to believe, by copying more closely the changes of place? We may presume not, since slow motion shows a body being carried along, floating among objects like seaweed, but not *moving itself*."[76] Merleau-Ponty thus emphasizes the *non-mimetic* feature of film realism—the ontological significance of such a remark is evident here—even without developing further his cinematic references.

However, Merleau-Ponty had lingered a bit longer on "the use of movement in painting and cinematic art"[77] in the summary of the first course he gave at the Collège de France, once again taking interest in their confluent features. It is the 1952–53 course devoted to "The Sensible World and the World of Expression," the preparatory notes for which have been transcribed and edited by Emmanuel de Saint Aubert[78] and by Stefan Kristensen.[79]

The reflections Merleau-Ponty provides in this course allow us to realize—or at least indicate more precisely—the directions by which the later phase of his thought could have developed an ontological conception of the cinema. Moreover, the notes prepared for the course "The Sensible World and the World of Expression" seem to support retrospectively the interpretation of the lecture Merleau-Ponty gave at the IDHEC as a silently polemic response to the Bergsonian judgment on cinema. In fact, just as in "The Cinema and the New Psychology," in these notes Merleau-Ponty discusses perception on the basis of the *Gestalttheorie*, and such a basis is used, this time explicitly, in order to reject Bergson's positions apropos of the cinema.

On the other hand, the summary of the same course already showed that Merleau-Ponty resorted to the *Gestalt* research in order to feed his opposition toward the Bergsonian thesis on movement, an opposition that seems to account for some of the allusions we found in the later rewritten chapter of *The Visible and the Invisible*. Indeed, in this summary, he explained what follows:

> [M]ovement as a change of location or variation in the relations between a "moving object" and its coordinates is a retrospective schema, an ulterior formulation of our carnal experience

of movement. Once it is cut off from its perceptual origins, movement defies representation and is self-destructive, as has often been shown since Zeno. But to give an intelligible account of movement is not enough to go back, as suggested by Bergson, to the internal experience of movement, in other words, to our own movement. We have to understand how the immediate unity of our gesture is able to spread over external experiences and introduce in them the possibility of transition that, from the standpoint of objective thought, is unreal.[80]

It is precisely when facing this question that Merleau-Ponty resorts to "the research in Gestalt theory."[81] And it is precisely when facing this question that, as I mentioned before, in the notes to the same course he critically echoes Bergson's positions on cinema in the light of Max Wertheimer's descriptions concerning stroboscopic movement. Wertheimer was the main Gestaltist theorist, and the stroboscopic movement he discussed is the apparent movement that is produced by the rapid succession of images on a background, which allows the viewer to perceive in a unitary way a cinematic sequence. But beware: according to Merleau-Ponty, such an experience cannot lead us to suppose any "movement without a moving object." This latter formulation, which is dismissed in the second part of the short reference to the cinema featured in the "appendix" of *The Visible and the Invisible*, is echoed several times in these 1952–53 course notes,[82] where it is indeed attributed to Wertheimer. In recalling the remarks already developed in *Phenomenology of Perception*, Merleau-Ponty considers such a formulation to be indefensible, at the risk of making the movement once more inconceivable, for in any case "he must be referring to an identical something that moves."[83] Therefore, these notes object, to Wertheimer no less than to Bergson, the exigency of a "theory of the perceiving body."[84] Indeed, only such a theory could attest to the "phenomenal truth of the movement" produced by "the discontinuous images of the cinema," hence showing us—this is the sense of the words we encountered in the short passage of the "appendix" to *The Visible and the Invisible*—that "the moving object could well be projected by him who perceives." Besides, this latter formulation, written in a subjectivist language, would be sufficient to explain Merleau-Ponty's decision not to publish this chapter. However, what is most important is to retain the Merleau-Pontian exigency of affirming, by the reference to corporeity, the immediate inscription of movement *both on the exterior and on the interior side of our experience.* For the same purpose, in the 1952–53 course notes, Merleau-Ponty uses the notion of "figural" in order to designate certain indecomposable features proper to *our perception* of a figure on a ground, and *not to the figure on the ground as such*, as the *Gestaltpsychologie* claimed. In short, he used this term so as to account for the essentially unitary characteristic of our experience of movement, while in his opinion "[t]he *Gestalt* turns figural moments into objective conditions, which determine a process of organization in the third person according to causality laws."[85]

Let us quote Kristensen, who refers to the notes he transcribed in order to explain that, according to Merleau-Ponty,

> [t]he structure of the stroboscopic movement coincides with that of our "natural perception." [. . .] There is an essential affinity between the functioning of our visual perception and the production of movement by cinematic technique. To support this idea, he indeed evokes cinema. The cinematic apparatus is "in no way illusion," he writes with reference to the well-known Bergsonian thesis of the *Creative Evolution* in the beginning of the fourth chapter. It must be admitted that [. . .] our body [. . .] shapes the perceived according to a structure that is its own.[86]

In order to support this thesis, Merleau-Ponty makes some direct references to one of the very rare movies he mentions in these course notes. More precisely, he refers to a specific sequence of *Zéro de conduite* (in English: *Zero for Conduct*), a masterpiece by the French film director Jean Vigo, which was issued on April 7, 1933, and was subsequently banned in France until 1945. The film is now considered as a classic and was particularly admired by the exponents of the *Nouvelle Vague*. Merleau-Ponty focuses on the famous sequence of the boys' nighttime rebellion in the dormitory of their boarding school. In the first part of this sequence, all the objects in the dormitory are thrown around as the children express their disdain for authority. Partway through the sequence, there is a shift to slow motion, as pillows and feathers fly and the children parade through the room. As Georges Sadoul observed, this sequence is remarkable "not only for its music, but also for the symphony in white major of its images."[87]

All of Merleau-Ponty's allusions to the sequence in his course notes are accompanied by the reference to a name in parenthesis: that of Maurice Jaubert. As I already reminded above, before World War II, Jaubert was the most important French composer of film music, and his reflections on "the role of music" in film were quoted by Merleau-Ponty in *The Film and the New Psychology*.[88] Jaubert also composed the music for *Zéro de conduite*. About the sequence quoted by Merleau-Ponty, Jaubert himself had explained what follows:

> The composer had to accompany a procession of rebellious children (quite ghostly in fact and shot in slow motion). Once the necessary music was obtained and wanting to use an unreal sonorousness, he transcribed it backwards, the last bar before the first and within each bar, the last note before the first. The bit of music in this form was then recorded and recalled little of the original music. The music thus obtained was then used with the film and one found again the shape of the basic melody but the "transmission" was entirely reversed and derived all its mystery from this simple mechanical operation.[89]

Merleau-Ponty's notes refer precisely to the effect produced at once by the reversal of the original music and the use of slow motion. Besides, his notes seem to echo Jaubert's explication itself, for they highlight in turn the "impression of irreality,"[90] of "strangeness [?]"[91] that the sequence causes in the spectator. We can hence understand Merleau-Ponty's interest in this sequence. In it, he sees a sort of negative proof, a sort of evidence to the contrary, showing the existence of a *logic shared* by our average perception and by the cinematic perception, despite Bergson's opinion according to which the latter was just an illusory reproduction of the former. By reversing the sounds and switching to slow motion, this sequence from *Zéro de conduite tries to elude* precisely that *perceptual logic*,[92] thus producing an effect of derealization. This is why, in the summary of Merleau-Ponty's course, we can read the following passage: "The quality of the sound from a wind instrument bears the mark and the organic rhythm of the breath from which it came, as can be shown by the strange impression received by reversing the normal register of the sounds. Far from being a simple 'displacement,' movement is inscribed in the texture of the shapes or qualities and is, so to speak, the revelation of their being."⁹³

There is more. When observing this sequence, it becomes evident that it is precisely to it that Merleau-Ponty will make reference, more or less eight years later, in the aforementioned passage from *Eye and Mind*, in which, talking about the cinematic expression of movement, he will claim—actually, a bit mysteriously—that "slow motion shows a body being carried along, floating among objects like seaweed, but not *moving itself*."⁹⁴ In the sequence in question, that body floating as seaweed appears, while its somersault slowly soars in the air as if that body itself were a feather. Or as if it were one of Bill Viola's angels.⁹⁵

Reread within the context of images and reflections that I just tried to recall, that sentence from *Eye and Mind* is then confirmed once and for all as a claim that, far from meaning to disavow the perception of movement offered by the cinema, rather criticizes the idea that the more such a perception is left to a close reproduction of movement itself, the more it is realistic. On the contrary, a close reproduction of movement cannot but distort the perceptual logic that immediately joins our body to the world. Therefore, our body will not recognize, in the projected

Figure 2.2. Jean Vigo, *Zéro de conduit*, 1933. Film still. © Argos Films.

slow motion movements of a similar body, the acting of its double. Rather, it will believe it is observing a way of dwelling in the world that is completely different from its own, as that of seaweed can be. It is thus precisely because this perceptual logic shows that we are joined to the world in an immediate and essential way, that it prevents us from separating the consideration of movement as we experience it and as it takes place in the world. Such a logic should even prevent us from describing it as a movement that is *within Being*, if by this expression we keep meaning that Being remains motionless. Indeed, as the Gestaltist experiments show and as the experiences of the cinema confirm, *the background essentially participates in the perception of movement*, obliging us to characterize such a movement not as movement *in* Being, but rather as movement *of* Being itself, which in its turn is revealed as *being movement*. This is precisely what the course notes in question end up pointing out: "Therefore here movement = revelation of Being, outcome of its internal configuration and clearly different from change of place."[96]

Hence, if the young Sartre claimed that the cinema raised a decisive problem for Western thinking, according to Merleau-Ponty, precisely the cinema helps indicate the direction to be followed in order to avoid the fundamental dualisms of the Western tradition. In this sense, the summary of the course on "The Sensible World and the World of Expression" proposes some reflections making the "use of movement" issue coincide not merely with a particular question, but with the very identity of what we heard Merleau-Ponty call, in a remarkable expression, "cinematic art."

Merleau-Ponty had already referred to the question of the cinema as art—a question whose deep philosophical importance we have already had the opportunity to measure thanks to the young Sartre—in one of his talks (*Causeries*) broadcast in 1948 on French radio:

> Cinema has yet to provide us with many films that are works of art from start to finish: its infatuation with stars, the sensationalism of the zoom, the twists and turns of plot and the intrusion of pretty pictures and witty dialogue, are all tempting pitfalls for films which chase success and, in so doing, eschew properly cinematic means of expression. While these reasons do explain why, hitherto, there have scarcely been any films that are entirely filmic, we can nevertheless get a glimpse of how such a work would look. We shall see that, like all works of art, such a film would also be something that one would perceive.[97]

Merleau-Ponty thus suggests judging films as "works of art from start to finish," provided that they are "entirely filmic," namely, that they avoid the flatteries of commercial success as much as those of other forms of expression, such as photography and literature, at the cost of their proper forms. In short, Merleau-Ponty suggests considering as "cinematic art" the cinema that is capable of being autonomous. In fact, the aforementioned passage continues as follows:

> Beauty, when it manifests itself in cinematography, lies not in the story itself, which could quite easily be recounted in prose and still less in the ideas which this story may evoke; nor indeed does it lie in the tics, mannerisms and devices that serve to identify a director, for their influence is no more decisive than that of a writer's favourite words. What matters is the selection of episodes to be represented and, in each one, the choice of shots that will be featured in the film, the length of time allotted to these elements, the order in which they are to be presented, the sound or words with which they are or are not to be accompanied. Taken together, all these factors contribute to forming a particular overall cinematographical rhythm. When cinema has become a longer-established facet of our experience, we will be able to devise a sort of logic, grammar, or stylistics, of the cinema which will tell us—on the basis of our knowledge of existing works—the precise weight to accord to each element in a typical structural grouping, in order that it can take its place there harmoniously."[98]

The reason why I decided to quote such a long passage drawn from the "*causerie*" titled "Art and the Perceived World" is that therein Merleau-Ponty shows a prominent interest in the question concerning what should be considered as "entirely filmic." Due to this interest, he points out the relevance of establishing, in the future, what he defines as a "stylistics of the cinema." In this light, it is even more interesting to mention the recent discovery of the film critic Marcel Martin's notes taken during a talk—concerning which no precise information had so far been collected—that Merleau-Ponty gave at the "Institut de Filmologie" in Paris on May 4, 1949, a few months after the broadcast of the aforementioned "*causerie*." In this talk, titled "La signification au cinema [The Meaning in Cinema],"[99] Merleau-Ponty attaches fundamental importance to cinema's stylistics, which is in turn connected to the question on how to define "the perfect film."

But let's go back to the passage from the aforementioned "*causerie*." In it Merleau-Ponty made clear that whatever is "entirely filmic" ends up aggregating in what he defines as "a particular overall cinematographical rhythm." Hence, this "overall cinematographical rhythm" cannot but embody the "use of movement" that is proper to what Merleau-Ponty, in the course theme of "The Sensible World and the World of Expression," calls "cinematic art."[100]

In this course theme, he indeed writes that "[t]he cinema, invented as a means of photographing objects in movement or as a *representation of movement*, has discovered in the process much more than change in location, namely a new way of symbolizing thoughts, a *movement of representation*."[101]

In this very "discovery" seems to reside, on the one hand, the cinema's feature of "art"—that is, the very nonmimetic feature Klee claimed for all art—and, on the other hand, its ontological novelty. Both these features are more explicitly justified a little farther, where Merleau-Ponty writes that "the film no longer plays with objective movements, as it did at first, but with *changes of perspective which define the shift from one person to another or his merging with the action*."[102]

It is also important to remark that, in the aforementioned sentence, Merleau-Ponty still uses the notion of "representation." However, it seems possible to affirm that the "discovery" defined in this sentence by the expression "movement of representation" is precisely what will lead him to abandon this notion so as to explore, in all its implications, that of "vision," by resolutely refusing to reduce it, as we have already seen, to an "operation of thought that would set up before the mind a picture or a *representation* of the world."[103]

Furthermore, it seems that the reasons for Merleau-Ponty's interest in André Bazin's reflections—which were only mentioned in the 1960–61 course notes—can hence be better understood. In fact, the theoretical convergence between the later Merleau-Ponty and Bazin seems to center around a new ontological consideration of vision and thus of the image.

Ontology of the Image as Figure of Mutual Precession

On this issue, in his 1945 article on "The Ontology of the Photographic Image," which is considered to be fundamental for the renewal of cinematic theories after World War II, in referring to the surrealist use of photography, Bazin wrote that "the logical distinction between what is imaginary and what is real tends to disappear. Every image is to be seen as an object, and every object as an image."[104]

In *Eye and Mind*, when reflecting on the novelties of modern painting, Merleau-Ponty claims in his turn that the image shall no longer be considered as "a tracing [*décalque*], a copy, a second thing,"[105] more or less faithful to its model, and anyway produced by a vision independent from our sensible relation to the world.

Just like in the coeval pages of the unfinished *The Visible and the Invisible*, here Merleau-Ponty thinks of the bodily experience as being constituted starting from the relational horizon of the flesh.[106] He thus means to affirm the *rising* of vision from the very "core" of such a horizon, rather than describing it as *striking out* from inside the body: "The visible about us seems to rest in itself. It is as though our vision were formed in the heart of the visible."[107]

Merleau-Ponty adds that what makes my vision rise at the core of the visible is the folding of the visible itself into a viewer. Indeed, in the same writing, Merleau-Ponty talks about "this *fold*, this central cavity of the visible which is my vision."[108] My experience of the body consists precisely in this "sort of folding back, invagination,"[109] a body experienced as a visible which is, at the same time, a viewer, as a sensible which is, at the same time, sentient. Such a condition is what makes me bear a relationship with the world that could be described as a kind of Möbius strip,[110] in virtue of which the sides traditionally defined as "inside" and "outside" trace the obverse and the reverse of the unique circle of vision.

Hence, in virtue of this circle, as Merleau-Ponty remarks in *Eye and Mind*, "we touch the sun and the stars [. . .] we are everywhere at once, and [. . .] even our power to imagine ourselves elsewhere [. . .] or freely to envision real beings, wherever they are, borrows from vision and employs means we owe to it."[111]

In fact, in relation to this characterization of vision, the imaginary can neither be conceived as a substituting faculty nor as a surrogate for reality; it does not express mere absence or total otherness with respect to the real. Rather, it turns out to germinate—precisely together with vision itself—from that *sensible kinship* between the world and us that, as we know, Merleau-Ponty calls *flesh*. From this perspective, he infers that the imaginary is much closer to the "actual [*actuel*]"[112] than a *copy* of the actual itself would be, because in the imaginary the resonance that the actual elicits in the flesh of our sensible, affective, and symbolic relationship with the world finds itself expressed.

Hence, Merleau-Ponty writes, once again in *Eye and Mind*, that the pictorial image should be regarded, in its relation to the field of the actual, as its "pulp and carnal obverse exposed view for the first time."[113] Still, can we avoid referring such a definition to the filmic experience itself?

At least, it is certain that Jean-Luc Godard cannot. In fact, in his film *JLG/JLG: Self-Portrait in December*, released in early 1995, he resorts to a few passages from a famous page of *The Visible and the Invisible*,[114] and assembles them in a *montage* resulting in a series of "phrases"—this is how the subtitle of the book released after the movie defines them—which I shall quote in its entireness:

> Sir / it's a film / that hasn't / ever been made / madam / it's a film / that nobody has seen / if my left hand / can touch my right hand / while it palpates / the tangibles / can touch it touching / why / when touching the hand of another / would I not touch / in it / the same power / to espouse the things / that I have touched / in my own / but this domain / one rapidly realizes / is unlimited / If we can / show that the flesh / is an ultimate notion / that it is not the union / or compound / of two substances / but thinkable by itself / if there is a relation / of the visible / with itself / that traverses me / and constitutes / me / as a seer / this circle / which I do not form / which forms me / this coiling over of the visible / upon the visible / can traverse / animate other bodies / as well / as my own / and if I was able to understand / how this wave arises / within me / how the visible / which is yonder is / simultaneously / my landscape / I can understand / *a fortiori* / that elsewhere / it also closes over / upon itself / and that there are other / landscapes / besides my own.[115]

Indeed, as Francesco Casetti points out in his book, significantly titled *Eye of the Century*,[116] cinema appears as the mode of expression that, being born in the same years as modern painting, has once and for all highlighted and made popular certain aspects of the "transformation in the relationship between humanity and Being"[117] that, in *Eye and Mind*, Merleau-Ponty sees precisely in modern painting. If, on the one hand, such relations can be negatively recognized in the refusal of the mimetic relation with the real, on the other hand, they seem to find a positive formulation in the definition of vision Merleau-Ponty provides in *Eye and Mind*, when he describes it as a "precession of what is upon what one sees and makes see, of what one sees and makes seen upon what is."[118]

I am, hence, going to focus on this strange and complex formulation, as I feel it is quite rich in important implications. The word *precession*—which will become more current in the language of the French poststructuralist generation[119]—is only used on this single occasion in Merleau-Ponty's so far published texts, but I shall warmly thank Emmanuel de Saint Aubert for providing me with the list of all the passages in which the word appears in Merleau-Ponty's still unpublished manuscripts.[120]

Indeed, it appears for the first time in his reading notes, which were probably taken in 1957, on Rudolf Arnheim's *Art and Visual Perception: a Psychology of the Creative Eye*, namely a book originally published in 1954,[121] where the word *precession*, however, was not mentioned. Later, it occurs several times in Merleau-Ponty's writings since 1960, starting with some drafts concerning the definition of vision from *Eye and Mind*, which I quoted above. On this basis, we can state that Merleau-Ponty seems to be interested in the word *precession* because it describes a *temporal* relation between the connected terms, rather than the *spatial* one suggested by the words *enjambement* and *empiétement*,[122] which, in those drafts, we find first put next to *precession* and then replaced by it.[123]

But the matter is not just Merleau-Ponty's preference for a temporal rather than a spatial relation. Indeed, the word *precession* describes a most peculiar temporality, which is characterized by a *movement of antecedence* of the concerned terms. Thus is the case with the precession of equinoxes, each of which happens about twenty minutes earlier each year.

Merleau-Ponty's preference for such a peculiar temporal relation becomes even more explicit in the unpublished "Large Summary" ["*Grand Résumé*"] of the *Visible and the Invisible* prepared between November 1960 and May 1961. In particular, here we find the word *precession* in the following note written in the fall of 1960: "Circularity, and *precession* visible-seer, silence-speech, I-Other [*moi-autrui*]."[124]

However, this formulation is significantly corrected in the following note from the same manuscript:

"Circularity, but rather *precession*   visible-seer
                                          Silence-speech
                                          I-Other [*moi-autrui*]."[125]

In this same page of the "Large Summary," Merleau-Ponty tries to explain the meaning of the word *precession* by another astronomical expression: "gravitation of one around the other."[126] Such an expression indeed suggests a mutual—even if spatial—relation between the connected terms.

As for the formulation of *Eye and Mind*, it makes explicit this aspect of *mutuality* in a *temporal* way, since *precession* is characterized here precisely by a *movement of mutual anticipation* of the terms implied in this relation. In fact, Merleau-Ponty specifies: "This precession of what is upon what one sees and makes seen, of what one sees and makes seen upon what is—this is vision itself." It is precisely due to this *mutuality of anticipation* that Merleau-Ponty uses the word *precession* to describe the interrelations between "what is" and "what one sees and makes seen," which, in his opinion, define vision. In short, Merleau-Ponty's definition concerns a kind of precession that cannot be but *mutual*: that is, the precession of the gaze with regard to the things and of the things with regard to the gaze; the precession of the imaginary with regard to the "actual"—since the imaginary deems our gaze *making us see* the actual—and the precession of the "actual" with regard to the imaginary. This is how the primacy of a term rather than the other—the things or the gaze, the imaginary or the actual—becomes undecidable. In other words, we end up discarding the possibility of recognizing, once and for all, which term *comes first* and which one has to be considered, to recall Merleau-Ponty's own expression, a "second thing." Besides, this should allow us to avoid keeping a "logical distinction"—this time the expression is Bazin's—between the movement and the mobile.[127]

In fact, the idea of mutual precession allows us to do without the notion of an absolute *before* in space and in time (or even a "before" *of* space and *of* time). Therefore, it reveals how much our way of *thinking* about reality as *absolutely prior* is still metaphysical, and invites us to consider it differently.

Let us try to accept this invitation. Evidently, this mutual precession is a retrograde movement digging a peculiar kind of depth in time. On the same issue, in *Eye and Mind*, Merleau-Ponty evokes the "immemorial depth [*fond*] of the visible."[128] I believe it is precisely in this sense that such a temporal depth is to be thought. On this subject, once again referring to the Proustian *Recherche*, in a working note of *The Visible and the Invisible* dated April 1960, Merleau-Ponty wrote: "The Freudian idea of the unconscious and the past as 'indestructible,' as 'intemporal' = elimination of the common idea of time as a 'series of *Erlebnisse*'—There is an architectonic past. cf. Proust: the *true* hawthorns are the hawthorns of the past [. . .].This 'past' belongs to a mythical time, to the time before time, to the prior life, 'farther than India and China.' "[129]

Moreover, in the manuscript of the same work he had already specified that this "mythical time" is the one "where certain events 'in the beginning' maintain a continued efficacy."[130] In my opinion, it is precisely the depth of this kind of time that is dug and instituted by the "precession of what is upon what one sees and makes seen, of what one sees and makes seen upon what is." Indeed, since this precession is infinitely mutual, it cannot bring us back to a chronological past. Rather, it can only bring us back to *a past that has never been present*, that is to say, a past which "belongs to a mythical time." This is the peculiar time at work in our unconscious, a time about whose indestructibility we read in the passage above. Similarly, "the indestructibility [. . .] the transformability, and the anachronism of the *events* of memory" characterize, according to Didi-Huberman, this temporality,[131] which will be therefore related to an involuntary memory as that evoked precisely by Proust. In other words, in this peculiar temporality the experiences of our life are involuntarily elaborated, by a sort of "active oblivion,"[132] as "carnal essences,"[133] as "sensible ideas."[134] Such ideas are mythically retrojected and sedimented as such through what Bergson called "the retrograde movement of the true," thus always remaining at work in that "architectonic past." As I tried to show elsewhere,[135] the mythical time is hence the peculiar time in which live what Merleau-Ponty calls the "sensible ideas," suggesting by such a name not only that these ideas are inseparable from their sensible presentation (that is, from their visual, linguistic, or musical images, for instance),[136] but even that they are *instituted* by these very images as their own depth. Therefore, these images share that mythical temporality in which such ideas live. Concerning this subject, let us read the following passage from *Eye and Mind*:

> Consider, as Sartre did in *Nausea*, the smile of a long-dead monarch which keeps producing and reproducing itself on the surface of a canvas. It is too little to say that it is there as an image or essence; it is there as itself, as that which was always most alive about it, the moment I look at the painting.[137] The "world's instant" that Cézanne wanted to paint, an instant long since passed away, is still hurled toward us by his paintings. His *Mont Sainte-Victoire* is made and remade

from one end of the world to the other in a way different from but no less energetic than in the hard rock above Aix.[138]

Even though we saw that later Merleau-Ponty's attention to cinema is explicitly focused on "the question of movement," I think that the mythical time, on which he reflects mainly apropos of the Proustian *Recherche*, is precisely *the time at work in the cinematic images.*[139] Without such time, cinema would have not provided the twentieth century with one of its most powerful myth systems and with its most popular place for psychoanalytic elaboration. More generally, it seems to me that the definition of vision elaborated by Merleau-Ponty in *Eye and Mind* ends up characterizing the status that the artistic experiences of the twentieth century gradually accorded to images,[140] that is to say, the status of *mutual precession figures* rather than merely *figures referring to something else*. Cinema, more than any other twentieth-century form of expression, has highlighted that status so much as to make it "enough to question the cleavage between the real and the imaginary."[141] From this perspective, the mutual precession of statements such as "it looks like a movie" and "it looks real" is emblematic. Still in the same perspective, cinema made familiar to us the paradoxical experience Merleau-Ponty describes apropos of painting in *Eye and Mind*: "I would be hard pressed to say where the painting is I am looking at. For I do not look at it as one looks at a thing, fixing it in its place [. . .]. Rather than seeing it, I see according to, or with it."[142]

Thus, if the image is not a "second thing," this is because of its mutual precession with "what is." And it is precisely because of this mutual precession that we see "according to, or with images.[143] Cinema has made the links among these three Merleau-Pontian formulations manifest in our experience, but we are just beginning to develop philosophy according to their implications and consequences.

All This Being Said:
Sartre, Merleau-Ponty, Deleuze, and the "Philosophy-Cinema"

First of all—and inevitably, but perhaps not wonderlessly—this analysis of some of the fundamental reflections on cinema undertaken by Sartre, Merleau-Ponty, and Deleuze leads to highlighting some important elements connecting them. As is well known, in the "Preface to the French edition" of *The Movement-Image*, Deleuze states that "the great directors of cinema may be compared, not merely with painters, architects and musicians, but also with thinkers."[144] It is a strange formulation, because it seems to imply that it is not evident to compare "painters, architects, musicians" with thinkers, as he suggests we should do with filmmakers. Deleuze certainly emphasizes that the thought of filmmakers has a specificity, which consists in being inseparable from cinematographic expression. Nevertheless, a similar claim could be made for all other forms of artistic practice, each expressing itself in a particular manner which is one and the same with its own manner of *thinking*.

Indeed, we know that Sartre sees in the cinematographic expression "symbolism [. . .] in its genesis," and that Merleau-Ponty sees in it ideas in their "nascent state," just like the aesthetic ideas for Kant (hence, bearing in turn a symbolic characteristic).[145] This way, both Sartre and Merleau-Ponty flag the importance of the novelty of cinematographic expression.[146] For his part, Deleuze affirms such a novelty by speaking, on the one hand, of "movement-images" (characterizing a cinema in which the symbolic feature of images intervenes mainly in a certain phase),[147] and, on the other hand, of "time-images." Indeed, all three thinkers refuse to refer to the word *concept*.[148]

Besides, it should be remarked that, at the time of the essays gathered in *Sense and Non-Sense*, Merleau-Ponty seemed to find that the artistic researches in the cinema and in Cézanne's painting were convergent with the philosophical researches of phenomenology, just as the young Sartre or the Deleuze of the cinema diptych had done with the philosophy of Bergson. In short, this shows how also Merleau-Ponty, rather than focusing on the "fundamental thought" at work in the cinema itself, was highlighting the historical convergence between the novelty of the cinema and that of his philosophy of reference.

It is necessary, however, to note that Merleau-Ponty's attitude seems to change in the final phase of his reflection, in which he uses precisely the expression "fundamental thought."[149] In fact, in this period, Merleau-Ponty ends up leaning on this kind of thought, namely the thought that operates in the domains that are supposed to be "nonphilosophical" (such as literature, painting, and cinema), because according to him they express a "spontaneous philosophy"[150] that he aims at making more explicit in order to better escape from what he names the "official philosophy facing a crisis."[151] It is during this time that the reasons for the change, which I pointed out above, in Merleau-Ponty's attitude become clearer. According to him, differently from what happened in the immediate second postwar period, among the researches that at the dawn of the 1960s gather their efforts to express what is the "transformation in the relationship between humanity and Being," philosophy ends up being out of place, for it remains cast away into categories of thought that condemn it to a radical "delay."[152] This is why we know that he himself comes to forge the word *a-philosophy*[153] as a way of developing a style of thought and expression having the concrete efficacy of "conceptless"[154] experiences and knowledge; such are the experiences and knowledges that are sedimented in certain images no less than certain modes of speech. Therefore, what Merleau-Ponty wrote concerning the latter can only be valid also concerning the former: "[T]he words most charged with philosophy are not necessarily those that enclose what they say, but rather those that most energetically open upon Being, because they more closely convey the life of the whole and make our habitual evidences vibrate until they disjoin."[155]

It is in this "a-philosophical" direction that Merleau-Ponty's interest in the aconceptual nature of Kantian "aesthetic ideas"—which we have seen evoked in order to characterize the cinematographic expression itself—turns into the theorization of Proustian "sensible ideas,"[156] on the subject of which he uses precisely the Kantian expression *conceptless*. Rather than a cohesion due to the fact that they "enclose what they say," he attributes to them "a *cohesion without concept*, which is of the same type as the cohesion of the parts of my body, or the cohesion of my body with the world."[157] Merleau-Ponty claims that, in the pages of the *Recherche* he makes allusion to, Proust characterizes an order of ideas that—just like aesthetic ideas for Kant—cannot be reduced to concepts, ideas that the intelligence, as such, cannot grasp, because—as Merleau-Ponty emphasizes—they "are without intelligible sun."[158] Indeed, he insists, "it is essential to this sort of ideas that they be 'veiled in darkness' "[159] and not let themselves "be erected into a second positivity"[160]—precisely the positivity that allowed concepts to encompass what they state—because we cannot "see [them] without the veils"[161] to the extent that it is these veils that make the ideas radiate.

More generally, it is a question of ideas that can only be *experienced*—because knowing them means *bodily* experiencing them—by encountering them in one of their sensible manifestations: encountering them on some kind of "screen" or of "veil" (here Merleau-Ponty interchangeably uses the two terms), even if only metaphorical, such as listening in the case of a piece of music or reading in that of a literary work. In any case, the presence of a surface of mediation proves decisive for this conceptless thought.

Regarding the cinema in particular, the direction of Merleau-Ponty's "a-philosophical" research just evoked seems to imply, notably, the reflection of André Bazin, given that the name of the latter is the only one that he cites in the context of this research.[162] We can consequently claim that, for the reasons I indicated up to this point, in the final period of his production he intended to elaborate a thought supplied by the "implicit philosophy" at work in reflections such as those of André Bazin.[163]

We could be tempted to say that Deleuze develops a similar operation to Merleau-Ponty's, for example at the beginning of *The Time-Image*, where he takes up and elaborates in an autonomous way the indications and the remarks that Bazin had dedicated to Italian neorealism.[164] Moreover, in an interview titled "On *The Time-Image*" Deleuze also claims that we can find in certain critical reflections on cinema a sort of "spontaneous philosophy": "Yet cinema critics, the greatest critics anyway, became philosophers the moment they set out to formulate an aesthetics of cinema. They weren't trained as philosophers, but that's what they became. You see it already in Bazin."[165]

Despite this element of convergence, we must note that the evolution of Deleuze's reflection concerning the relations between philosophy and the cinema seems to go in a direction opposed to that of the evolution of Merleau-Ponty's own thought. Indeed, the latter comes to give himself a task similar to the one Deleuze flags apropos of the philosophy of "today" already in the conclusion of the Preface of *Difference and Repetition* that I quoted at the beginning of this book: "The search for new means of philosophical expression."

On the other hand, fifteen years after the publication of this work, the assertion of the Preface of *The Movement-Image* mentioned above—according to which "the great directors of cinema [. . .] think with movement-images and time-images instead of concepts"[166]—shows the tendency to revive the identity of philosophy as a conceptual knowledge. This tendency is confirmed in the very final pages of *The Time-Image*.[167] Of course, there Deleuze emphasizes that it is necessary to understand "philosophical theory" as "a practice of concepts"; and, of course, he clarifies that "the theory of cinema is not about the cinema, but about the concepts of cinema." Nevertheless, he asserts that it is "the great directors of cinema [. . .] who speak the best about what they do"—a highly disputable claim, because it seems to ignore the hermeneutic principle concerning "what the author does not know."[168] Yet more contestable, he suggests that *they speak of their work through concepts*—he who, however, tells us that they "think with movement-images and time-images." Indeed, to him, precisely such "concepts of cinema" can be grasped by philosophy, understood as the practice of concepts, as its very "object," as he wrote in accordance with the most traditional approaches.[169]

We can thus wonder: What happened to the "philosophy-cinema"? How about this hyphen? If we leave behind the theoretical stake expressed by this hyphen—making "a philosophy-cinema"—do we not risk writing, once again, books of philosophy "as it has been done for so long," to speak with Deleuze himself, simply taking "the concepts of cinema," rather than cinema itself, for their *object*?

In order to avoid this risk, it would hence be necessary to radically develop the problematization of the ideas of "philosophy" and of "concept" that Deleuze had undertaken in the course of the 1960s,[170] which might mean, in its turn, exploring the history of the very notion of concept. We might observe that the modern conception of the latter is modeled on the German term that designates it, namely, the term *Begriff*, the roots of which refer to the gesture of "grasping" (*greifen*). Additionally, in such a conception we might be able to see the product of a process of *abstraction* from the notion of Idea established by Plato himself: this process consists in the separation and opposition of the essence and the existence, of the intelligible and the sensible, of the universal and the particular, and it marks the manner of thinking that we call *Platonism*, which continually dominates Western culture. Furthermore, this process of *abstraction* of the notion of Idea was at the same time the process of its *reification*, that is to say, its transformation into a positive entity, a sort of object. Of course, this is an "ideal object," but, as such, ideally graspable—as the German etymology of the term *concept* suggests—in all the domains of our experiences that philosophy claims to define: such as (the concepts of) cinema, for example.

In conclusion, in order to avoid such a risk it might be necessary to fully develop the program of *reversing Platonism*, which is the title of a famous 1967 text by Deleuze republished in the appendix to *The Logic of Sense*,[171] precisely the book of 1969 in which the author's "Note to the Italian edition" posits, as we saw, the notion of "philosophy-cinema." On the contrary, in the first half of the 1980s, when Deleuze devoted himself to his two books on cinema, his research seems to have left behind the intention of radically problematizing philosophy as conceptual knowledge, and it finishes by leaving open also the question concerning that which is ultimately "a philosophy-cinema." Perhaps it is this modified theoretical horizon which also explains the implicit criticism that Slavoj Žižek puts to the Deleuzian reflection on cinema: that it does not fully understand the philosophical importance of Alfred Hitchcock.[172] Or, as Merleau-Ponty would have said, the "spontaneous philosophy" at work in his films. Žižek's criticism of Deleuze is summarized when he reproaches Deleuze for not having seen that "*Vertigo* is, in a sense, the ultimate anti-Platonic film, a systematic materialist undermining of the Platonic project, akin to what Deleuze does in the appendix to *The Logic of Sense*."[173] In short, Žižek reproaches Deleuze for not having seen that the cinema of Hitchcock, and *Vertigo* in particular, can contribute effectively to the effort of *reversing Platonism*, which he encouraged fifteen years earlier. In the conclusion of *The Time-Image*, Deleuze shows, instead, the tendency to come back to a model of philosophy as *subject that must think of its objects*: "Cinema itself is a new practice of images and of signs, of which philosophy must make the theory."[174] Ah! the old style . . .

3

The Torn Curtain

Lyotard, the Screen, and a Cinema Named Desire

For an Ontological Rehabilitation of the Screen

In the reflections Merleau-Ponty consecrates to the cinema, we have seen a programmatic attention to *appearance*—after which phenomenology itself is named—conjugated with and supplied by the fundamental consideration of the *whole* that leads the *Gestalttheorie* to affirm the indecomposable feature of the perceived phenomena. On the one hand, this pushes such reflections toward perception meant as a *montage* realized according to the particular logic that bonds our body to the world; on the other hand, this imposes increasingly deep critical instances against metaphysics understood as a thought that situates the true *beyond* appearance itself. Such kind of instances lead Merleau-Ponty's later reflection to try to conceive the giving of the true not according to the traditional opposition—fixed by Plato in the Allegory of the Cave—between the deceiving shadows of appearances and the pure light emanated by truth, but rather on the basis of the quintessential complementarity of light and shadow. "A new idea of light: truth is itself *zweideuting* [. . .]. The *Vieldeutigkeit* is not a shadow to be eliminated from true light."[1]

Evidently, this cannot but suggest an *ontological rehabilitation of the surface on which appearance shows itself*. Such a surface shall no longer be thought as a *veil* that would conceal the true and that shall hence be removed or even pierced. Rather, it shall be considered as a *screen* that—just as in the case of the figure-ground relation or in the perception of the stroboscopic movement[2]—reveals itself to be the decisive condition to *make seen*, in its constitutive "ambiguity"—the truth of experience.

Still, it has to be remarked that, in Merleau-Ponty's thought, such a rehabilitation is insufficiently pointed out in at least two decisive aspects. As I noted in the last pages of the previous chapter, the first aspect has to do with the fact that he tends to talk alternatively about "screen" and "veil" (it is precisely with regard to the sensible *veil* capable of making visible certain ideas that we heard Merleau-Ponty claim that "there is no vision without the *screen*."[3]) Here emerges his tendency to assimilate the functions of showing typical of the screen and the veil, without differentiating their respective features, that is to say, without identifying them either with *completely* or with *partially* opaque surfaces, even if their positioning with relation to the luminous source and to the spectator is due precisely to this differentiation.[4] The second aspect concerns the historical or nonhistorical feature of their functions of showing. Such a historical feature is indeed sometimes suggested by Merleau-Ponty in connection with the rising of cinema. Yet, on other occasions, it is faded into a more generic consideration, as is the case with the emphasis he puts on the importance of the veil in his interpretation of Proust's "sensible ideas."

Despite such aspects, it remains evident that Merleau-Ponty aims at fulfilling an ontological rehabilitation of the surface of mediation so as to introduce the trend affirmation of a different way of conceiving the *giving* of the true, which, from a *theatrical* configuration—that is to say absolutely *representative*, inaugurating with the opening of the curtain—seems to switch to a *cinematic* configuration, hence dictating the aforementioned need of a philosophy-cinema.

In turn, the ontological rehabilitation of such a surface—which leads to considering the screen or the veil as the condition of the possibility of vision—can only be one and the same with the "new idea of light" understood as inseparable from the shadow, for only a similar surface may precisely *make visible* the truth of their common and mutual appearance.

Previously, we had noticed that Merleau-Ponty's thought goes so far as to abandon the notion of *representation*; instead, he explores that of *vision*. Now, in the light of the considerations above, we can add that it is precisely starting with vision that, in the early 1970s, the thought of Jean-François Lyotard was urged, for its part, to part from phenomenology understood in its Merleau-Pontian "acclimatization."[5] The important programmatic text in which Lyotard explains the reasons for his separation from phenomenology is the reelaboration of his PhD thesis. Its title is *Discourse, Figure*, and it was published in 1971.[6]

The Bias of Desire

From their very title, the pages of the introduction to *Discourse, Figure* announce "[t]he Bias of the Figural." We had already seen Merleau-Ponty indicate, by this notion, certain properties that are intrinsic to our perception of a figure. Lyotard uses it to designate the domain of the visible, which, still according to Merleau-Ponty's teaching, can only give itself together with its double chiasm with the visual on the one hand,[7] and with the invisible on the other hand. Such a domain—he explains—doubtlessly constitutes certain "figures" in the "discourse," but remains irreducible to the latter in virtue of its own "opacity." In other words, the figural is determined, according to Lyotard, as "the inclusion of an illegal mobility in the linguistic order."[8] A little farther on, he still points out that the figural "deconstructs not only discourse but the figure, inasmuch as the figure is a recognizable image or a regular form."[9] Then he adds: "And underneath the figural: difference. Not just the trace, not just presence-absence, indifferently discourse or figure, but the primary process, the principle of disorder, the incitement to *jouissance*. Not some kind of interval separating two terms that belong to the same order, but an utter disruption of the equilibrium between order and non-order."[10]

Here we start measuring the distance that Lyotard puts between himself and Merleau-Ponty. For the latter, language "*metamorphoses the structures of the visible world*,"[11] which means that he conceives language both as a decentering *and a restructuring* of the visible world. Lyotard, for his part, describes processes of "absolute" disordering, and, as I mentioned before, he highlights the irreducibility of the discourse and of the figure. Indeed, in his conception of the figural, Lyotard understands the visible not only as a "recognizable image"—which, as we saw, in his opinion is itself likely to be disrupted—but also as a phantom, a hallucination, for he thinks that "[w]e reach here the limits of a phenomenological interpretation: with hallucination, we move beyond the sensible."[12] Indeed, for Lyotard what is at work in the figural is not perception, but *desire*.

In this way, he refers (and reduces) the notion of vision, as explored by the later Merleau-Ponty, to a strictly (and narrowly) perceptual domain[13]—the only one that he finds pertinent to phenomenology—and claims, for vision in itself, an essential bond to desire. Thus, he affirms that a philosophy that tries to think of vision in such terms needs to reach out for something that he does not feel phenomenology is capable of approaching.

In 1973, in the aftermath of *Discourse, Figure*, Lyotard published two collections of essays: *Dérive à partir de Marx et de Freud* and *Des dispositifs pulsionnels*.[14] Thanks to some of these essays, the topic of desire explicitly appears in the French philosophical reflection on cinema. Indeed, in the 1970 essay titled "Notes on the Critical Function of the Work of Art," originally published in the *Revue d'Esthétique* and appearing in the first of the two collections, Lyotard remarks: "It is obvious that the image—notably in cinema—[. . .] begins to function as a scene in which my desire is caught and comes to fulfilment. This can happen, for example, in the form of the projection into the characters or the situations."[15]

It is precisely starting with these premises that, in the other collection of essays, Lyotard published his "first important text on cinema,"[16] titled "Acinema," which had already appeared that same year in the *Revue d'Esthétique*.[17] Of course, in this text the attention to the topic of desire does by no means *replace* that to the specificity of the "use of movement" that, as we saw, characterizes the cinema. On the contrary, the *incipit* of Lyotard's article is in full continuity with such a direction: "Cinematography—he explains by alluding to the etymology of this term—is the inscription of movement, a writing with movements—all kinds of movements."[18] It is, however, movement itself that is understood as desire by Lyotard, who recalls on this subject the linguistic bond between *emotion* and *motion*.[19] In this sense, the article shows in a particularly efficient way Lyotard's attempt to part from phenomenology and from its presumed limits.

Specular Wall, Plastic Screen, Cinematic Screen

From this standpoint, the way of characterizing the screen is emblematic. We have seen that in Merleau-Ponty this characterization is first of all, yet not exclusively, perceptual. For his part, in the "Acinema," Lyotard presents it by means of a parallel with the determination of the mirror posited by Jacques Lacan: "Film acts as the orthopedic mirror analyzed by Lacan in 1949 as constitutive of the imaginary subject or *objet a*; that we are dealing with the social body in no way alters its function."[20]

Actually, in the communication he delivered at the XVI International Congress on Psychoanalysis on July 17, 1949,[21] Lacan had determined the "mirror stage" as an "*identification*"[22] with a primordial form of the "I" [*Je*] (rather than with a "subject"), and this without ever mentioning the notion of *objet a*, which he will develop later (outlining it with precision in 1964 also thanks to the posthumous publication of Merleau-Ponty's *The Visible and the Invisible*).[23] Besides, contrarily to what Lyotard claims, this notion does not aim at designing any "identifications," but rather, as Slavoj Žižek explains, "the part of our image that eludes the mirrorlike symmetrical relationship."[24] In any case, the point of Lacan's communication that draws Lyotard's interest seems to be that which "situates the agency known as the ego, prior to its social determination, in a fictional direction."[25] From here, Lyotard draws the analogy between the *infans'* body and the social body on the one hand, and the mirror function and the cinematic screen on the other hand.[26] On the basis of such an analysis, he hence sets a fundamental objective for his reflection on the cinema: "We will have to ask ourselves how and why the *specular wall* in general, and thus the cinema screen in particular, can become a privileged place of the libidinal cathexis."[27]

Another text included in *Des Dispositifs pulsionnels* helps outline at least a few aspects of what he considers as "the *specular wall* in general": that is, "Freud According to Cézanne."[28] By highlighting that Cézanne's painting features a "principle of derepresentation,"[29] Lyotard admits that "Merleau-Ponty was entirely correct to make this principle the core of the work in its entirety."[30] Still, he claims that Merleau-Ponty's interpretation was limited to considering this principle as being at work *in the domain of perception*, so as to "rediscover the true order of the sensible."[31] On the contrary, Lyotard sees in it the symptom of a "veritable displacement of the desire of painting,"[32] a displacement such as to end up disrupting the very function of painting, which, starting with the *Quattrocento*, had been precisely *"function* of [. . .] *representation."*[33] Besides, for Lyotard, Freud's psychoanalysis was no more successful in noticing this "displacement of [. . .] desire" in the pictorial domain, which could have provided one of the most emblematic expressions of the more general mutation of desire that took place in the West precisely starting with the last part of the nineteenth century. Indeed, by referring in particular to *Leonardo da Vinci and a Memory of His Childhood*,[34] Lyotard claims that Freud, in his reflections on painting, has continued to think of the painter's canvas—which Lyotard, for his part, qualifies as a "plastic screen"—"in accordance with the representative function," by considering it "as a transparent support behind which an inaccessible scene unfolds."[35]

As Lyotard openly says in a talk on "Painting and Desire," delivered at the Sorbonne in 1972 such a characterization of the "plastic screen" as a "transparent support" clearly refers to the theoreticians of the Renaissance perspective, who, starting with Leon Battista Alberti, had characterized such a screen "as a window opening onto a view, onto a scene that would be out there, on the other side,"[36] hence officially inaugurating the historical process by which the window has become the optical apparatus that the modern times have assumed as their model of vision.[37]

However, focusing on Freud, we could state that, still according to Lyotard, he considered the "plastic screen" as a sort of *veiled window*, rather than transparent,[38] that is to say a window concealed by a *curtain*, which, *on the one side*, could *hide* the truth of an "inaccessible scene," and, *on the other side*, could *show* the representation and provide desire with an illusionary fulfillment. In turn, this curtain whose function is constitutively double-sided, appears to me as a (historically determined) variant of what, in the "Acinema," Lyotard names "*specular wall* in general," and which I think he considers as a feature common to the pictorial and the cinematic screen. Indeed, this double-sided function that I just described is unified in the most current signification of the word *screen*: *on the one side, to hide, on the other side, to show*.

As I mentioned before, "Freud According to Cézanne" contests Freud as, according to Lyotard, he persisted in an interpretation of painting understood as representation even in the historical moment in which painting itself was losing its representative function—which, in any case, in the "Acinema," Lyotard still considered to be the largely dominant function of images. However, the first essay claims that Freud had continued to think of the (pictorial) *screen as a (veiled) window*, and, consequently, that he had continued to think of images themselves as "screens" that one would have to metaphysically "rent."[39] On the contrary, Lyotard highlights that, precisely starting with the same historical moment, "[t]he critical work began by Cézanne, continued or reengaged in all directions by Delaunay and Klee, by the cubists, by Malevitch and Kandinsky, attested that it was no longer at all a question of producing a phantasmatic illusion of depth on a screen treated like a window, but on the contrary of making visible plastic properties (lines, points, surfaces, values, colors) which representation only serves *to efface*; that it was therefore no longer a question of fulfilling desire through its delusion, but of capturing it and of methodically disappointing it by exposing its machinery."[40]

It is within this process, as Lyotard describes it, that he formulates his judgment on "the American Abstract expressionists of the period before *Pop art*,"[41] who, in his opinion, realize "that even the cubist space is still a space of depth [. . .] they reduce this deep space, which is still in some respects illusory because it is a screen within which desire can be lured, to a strictly two-dimensional space upon which expanses of color will be painted."[42]

The A-Art, the Acinema, and the Mutation of Desire

The intentions and the characteristics of this process end up positing the notion of "anti-art" that Lyotard borrows from Duchamp, but which immediately afterward he rather qualifies as "a-art."[43] This process aims at *deconstructing representation by unveiling its "machinery"* and hence at avoiding the illusionary fulfilment of desire by the fantasy (which is, as such, bonded to a prohibition),[44] so as to second and promote at once a "displacement of desire." On this subject, in the "Notes on the Critical Function of the Work of Art," he writes that "[t]here is, in modern art, a presence [. . .] in desire of the death drive."[45] This is why, in his opinon, the "displacement" of desire seems to consist in the switch from the search for pleasure to that for *jouissance*: "If you look at one of the most effective works of pop art, it exactly satisfies the conditions of sexual climax [*jouissance*], [. . .] This corresponds to the definition that, after Freud, orgasm [*jouissance*] must be given: the collaboration of Eros and death, the seeking of the most complex, the most differentiated organization, and its destruction."[46]

These remarks may authorize us to see a "displacement of desire" of the same kind at work in the Lyotardian notion of *acinema*, which is an analog of that of *a-art*.[47] As the essay on the acinema explains, "the acinema [. . .] would be situated at the two poles of the cinema taken as a writing of movements: thus, extreme immobilization and extreme mobilization."[48]

Besides, in the previous pages of the same essay, Lyotard had remarked that "these two seemingly contradictory currents appear to be those attracting whatever is intense in painting today."[49] If, hence, Lyotard unifies under the name of *acinema* these two currents in the cinematic domain, it is because both—either by slow motion or by acceleration of the perceived movement on the screen—make such movement appear as "nonnatural." They thus detach—at least as a trend—from the dominant current of the cinema, that is, its mainstream, namely, the cinema meant as a "representational narrative art."[50] This mainstream, for its part—similarly to what we have said about the dominant current in painting, and following the thesis of "Freud According to Cézanne"—will "efface" its very "support"[51] and in this way reveal itself as subject to the most traditional position of desire.[52] However, similarly to what, according to Lyotard, happens in abstract painting, in the acinema "the represented ceases to be the libidinal object while the screen itself, in all its most formal aspects, takes its place."[53] Lyotard expresses this very idea in his "Notes on the Critical Function of the Work of Art" by referring to Alain Resnais's film *Je t'aime, je t'aime* (France, 1968): "[the spectator's] desire collides with the screen, because the screen is treated as a screen and not as a window [*vitre*]. In the case of this film, the critical reversal is brought about by its cutting and editing [*montage*]."[54] However, in the case of the acinema *stricto sensu*, such a "critical reversal" would be performed by intervening in movement.[55]

In short, the "mutation of desire"[56] at once discerned and wished for by Lyotard in our epoch, by preventing us from recognizing and identifying ourselves in what is represented, instead of producing a form of pleasure consisting in the illusory fulfillment of desire itself, would rather tend to *make seen* the illusory feature of this very form of pleasure, mixing it with a deception in the *jouissance*, and hence implying a mutation of the status of the surface—the specular wall—which usually supports the illusion: namely, the screen. Lyotard's aforementioned reference[57] to the same formulation we found in Merleau-Ponty—*to make seen*—should be remarked, but at the same time, it should not deceive us. Of course, for both thinkers, the image hence shows itself as not being "a second thing,"[58] to echo another Merleau-Pontian formulation. In this sense, the ontological rehabilitation of the surface on which appearance shows itself—which I evoked at the beginning of this chapter by referring to Merleau-Ponty's thought—is prolonged by Lyotard's own thought. Still, if, on the one hand, this formulation couldn't but point out, being such a surface at stake, the condition *to make seen*, for the same reason, on the other hand, it becomes the surface that is *to be made seen*. If one looks deeper, this is precisely "the bias of the figural."

The Screen to Make Seen, the Screen to Be Made Seen: A Comparison Between Merleau-Ponty and Lyotard

Let us insist on the comparison between the two philosophers. We may remember that in his essay on the "acinema," Lyotard illustrates such a notion by the following example: "In *Joe* (a film built entirely upon the impression of reality) the movement is drastically altered twice: the first time when the father beats to death the hippie who lives with his daughter; the second when 'mopping up' a hippie commune he unwittingly guns down his own daughter. This last sequence ends with a freeze-frame shot of the bust and face of the daughter who is struck down in full movement. In the first movement we see a hail of fists falling upon the face of the defenceless hippie who quickly loses consciousness. These two effects, the one an immobilization, the other an excess of mobility, are obtained by waiving the rules of representation which demand real motion recorded and projected at 24 frames per second."[59]

In his book on cinema and the thought of Lyotard, Jean-Michel Durafour implicitly indicated another example of "acinema," precisely in the sequence that we found mentioned also in Merleau-Ponty's course notes for "The Sensible World and the World of Expression," namely, the sequence of the dormitory rebellion in *Zéro de conduite*.[60] This coincidence is in no way fortuitous. On the contrary, it is most significant. Indeed, if one looks deeper, the questions making Merleau-Ponty evoke that sequence and those making Lyotard evoke the scene of the hippie girl's murder are not unalike: How does it happen that the slow motion in the first and the immobilized images in the latter similarly suspend the spectators' spontaneous tendency of identifying with the *movement* of the images projected on the screen, hence producing an effect of uncanniness [*étrangeté*]? We already know Merleau-Ponty's answer: it is because the sequence of *Zéro de conduite*, slow-motioned and accompanied by notes played backward, contravenes our perceptual logic. Lyotard's answer, for its part, seems to be the following: it is because such "freeze-frame shots" appear, at least for a moment, to be preventing "the sparse drives," as he calls them, to recognize "an object where they can unite."[61] Such an answer is hence based on the parallel between the screen and the (Lacanian) mirror. However, isn't a similar parallel implied in Merleau-Ponty's own answer?[62] In *Eye and Mind*, he seems to evoke once more the sequence of the dormitory rebellion from *Zéro de conduite*, when writing that "slow motion shows a body being carried along, floating among objects like seaweed, but not *moving itself*."[63] Well, isn't such a body, floating like seaweed, at work precisely as an *objet a*? One may object that Merleau-Ponty refers it to "the One of perception," rather than to "the Id of desire,"[64] to recall the terms of *Discourse, Figure*. Yet, is it really possible to radically separate them? In any case, what is certain is that in this way one risks metaphysically placing desire *beyond the sensible*, as it indeed happens in Lyotard's text.

Still, influenced by Lacan's thought—which can also be traced in the later Merleau-Ponty—Lyotard wishes to point out, in turn, that "reality" is not a *primum*, but that it is organized by the very "staging" that produces its very representation.[65] This also allows understanding why and how Merleau-Ponty and Lyotard have both tried to rehabilitate the pictorial and cinematic screen, and to provide the latter with a characterization that could match the mutation both philosophers unconcealed in the arts of our epoch. Indeed, such arts seem to question the representative models of the theatre and of the window, which characterized our modernity, and which were both focused on the idea of a *curtain* whose metaphysical implications were multiple. The comparative look at Merleau-Ponty and Lyotard hence raises the *crucial problem* of the triple link binding the historicity of vision, the changing of optical apparatus assumed as the model of vision in a certain epoch, and the mutation of desire. When one looks deeper, the least we can say is that this triple link contributes to constituting the knot of the philosophy-cinema.

Yet, What "Mutation of Desire"?

Today more than ever, it is hence urgent to question at least on this triple link. On this subject, we heard Lyotard affirm that *"since the 1880s"*[66] Western culture would have faced a mutation for which "[i]n painting the emergence of a strange desire becomes visible: that the painting [. . .] be valued as an absolute object, relieved of the transferential relation."[67] More generally, starting with those years, a mutation of desire would have been at work progressively dissolving the system of representation based on the conception of the object as a symbol bearing a referential value. Such a dissolution would be evident "say for Western Europe over the last 15 years," Lyotard writes in his essay on Cézanne written in the early seventies.[68]

What Lyotard will define, at the end of the same decade, as *The Postmodern Condition*[69] would hence only be the extreme yet coherent product of the transformations that, in his mind, found their first pictorial expression in the work of Paul Cézanne. Indeed, if it is true that the transition to "what is known as the postmodern age [. . .] has been under its way since at least the end of the 1950s, which for Europe marks the completion of reconstruction,"[70] then it is also true that he interprets such a transition as a consequence of the "transformations which, since the end of the nineteenth century, have altered the game rules for science, literature, and the arts."[71]

The modern painter's desire to "disappoint," which Lyotard pointed out in his "Freud According to Cézanne,"[72] would hence prepare the "grief" and the "wise melancholy"[73] that he considers typical of our postmodern condition, as noted in the catalogue of the exhibition Les *immatériaux*, by which, in 1985, he tried to "make sensible"[74] the links between such a condition and the newborn electronic revolution.

On the other hand, we could remark that Lyotard also suggests a continuity, in the Western culture of the late nineteenth and twentieth century, between the dominant conception of painting, bonded to the Renaissance perspective, and the dominant trend of the cinema—whose birth yet happened a few years *after* the beginning of the aforementioned mutation of desire. Precisely this continuity of representation in both painting and cinema motivates, according to him, the continuity he observes between the "critical work" of modern painting (which, as we know, he qualifies as "a-art") and that of the "acinema," insofar as the latter continuity cannot but be *complementary to the first* since it needs it precisely in order to make a critical work on it.[75]

In other words, when highlighting the historical mutation of desire, Lyotard does not see a comparable mutation in the "emergence"[76] of cinema, that is to say, in the advent of the cinematic screen next to the "plastic" screen (namely, the painter's canvas). More exactly, Lyotard does not see, in this advent *as such*, a mutation capable of transforming the way in which each screen (pictorial and cinematic) incarnates what he calls "the *specular wall* in general." Eventually, in his opinion, the mutation of desire is what produces the critical work of modern painting and of the acinema *within* the dominant system of representation. In short, such a mutation would happen—once more in a way that cannot be qualified but in metaphysical terms—"beyond" perception.

Hence, for Lyotard as well as for a number of coeval film scholars, the advent, in our culture, of the screen placed in a dark theater, when compared to the pictorial canvas displayed in a room full of light, would not produce a historical mutation of the model of our vision.[77] This model would *remain* that of the Albertian window, and it would be, in the case both of the canvas and of the screen, subjected to the same "representative-narrative" conception of art.[78]

As for me, I think that a continuity between the perception modeled by the perspective of the Renaissance and the optics of cinema is undeniable. However, it is important to point out that actually our vision does not provide us with an "optical" access to the world, but rather with a "bodily" access to it. This means that the visual dominance of such an access to the world does not exclude its essentially *synaesthetic*[79] feature. Evidently, such a feature is not configured in the same way in the case of painting and in that of cinema.

Thus, is it possible to affirm that the window remains the optical apparatus assumed as a model of vision by our epoch?

The theoretical position I have defended so far by considering desire and perception as inseparable from one another can only lead to regard the mutation of the former and the mutation of the latter as, in turn, inseparable from one another, and both, again, as inseparable from the spreading of various *technologies* of perception and expression, since "each technology not only differently *mediates* our figurations of bodily existence but also *constitutes* them. That is, each offers our lived bodies radically different ways of 'being-in-the-world.' "[80]

In the very essay this quote is drawn from, Vivian Sobchack recurs to the thesis of a text in which Fredric Jameson, five years after Lyotard, had also tried to sketch out an analysis of postmodernism.[81] Jameson characterized it as the "cultural logic" emerging with the third stage of the history of capitalism—that of our time. In his opinion, such a stage should be qualified as "multinational capital," and it has been developing since the 1940s and 1950s. Before the postmodern phase, the "cultural periodization" posited by Jameson in parallel to the stages of capitalism includes the phase of "realism," beginning between the 1840s and the 1850s, and that of "modernism," beginning with the 1890s. For her part, Vivian Sobchack suggests also situating at the core of the three phases of Jameson's "cultural periodization" "three correspondent technological modes and institutions of visual (and aural) representation: respectively, the photographic, the cinematic, and the electronic."[82]

It is indeed remarkable to observe that, globally speaking, the second and third phase of this "cultural periodization" correspond more or less exactly to the ones indicated by Lyotard. It is even more remarkable to notice that, differently from Lyotard, Jameson's periodization, which Sobchack refers to and integrates with new content, reckons an active role for the cinema as such in the correlative historical mutations, just as it reckons an active role for photography and electronics. Indeed, Sobchack explains that each "has been critically complicit not only in a specific *technological revolution* within capital but also in a specific *perceptual revolution* within the culture and the subject. That is, each has been significantly co-constitutive of the particular temporal and spatial structures and phenomeno-logic that inform each of the dominant cultural logics Jameson identifies as realism, modernism, and postmodernism."[83]

This point leads to also question the characterization of desire in the postmodern time as it has been posited by Lyotard: Is it really a desire of deception that is one and the same with the affective tonality of "chagrin" and "wise melancholy"?

In his book titled *How to Read Lacan*, Žižek explains that, from the point of view of Freud's psychoanalysis, "the melancholic [. . .] is [. . .] the subject who possesses the object, but has lost his desire for it, because the cause that made him desire this object has retreated and lost its efficiency."[84] Such a definition seems to perfectly apply to the West of the postmodern epoch. Indeed, the object that caused its desire—an object that could be named "the world"—seems to have been completely dominated, but at the same time it has become an object without a cause, since "God is dead" and the world has lost its enchantment, which was due to its reference to a "beyond."[85]

A similar object hence functions "as an autonomous organ without body, located in the very heart of my body and at the same time uncontrollable,"[86] which thus becomes "the source of shame."[87] This is precisely what happens to the West today: the object that used to urge its desire, by now deprived of its cause, has become a sort of "organ without a body" producing, in the very body of the West, the autoimmune syndrome that emerged emblematically on 9/11,[88] and which, contrarily to what Lyotard thought, is no "wise" at all. Today, it is clear that the suicide trend manifested by such a syndrome seeks for dizziness in an unbridled run for enjoyment [*jouissance*], which, as we will see in the second part of the present book, finds its "mythical time" in the present and its "mythical space" in the contemporary screens.

Part Two

The Animated Life of Screens

I tried [. . .] to clear what the average and profane public could feel when facing the screen.

—Jean-Paul Sartre, "Apologie pour le cinema"

4

Delimiting to Exceed

The Theme of the "Arche-Screen" Founding Itself with Its Variations

The Screen, the Canvas, the Window

> Let us compare the screen [*Leinwand*] on which a film unfolds with the canvas [*Leinwand*] of a painting. The image on the film screen changes, whereas the image on the canvas does not. The painting invites the viewer to contemplation; before it, he can give himself up to his train of associations. Before a film image, he cannot do so. No sooner has he seen it than it has already changed. It cannot be fixed on.[1]

This is how in the fourteenth chapter of the second typed version[2] of *The Work of Art in the Age of Its Technological Reproducibility*, Walter Benjamin urges us to make the comparison that will occupy most of the present chapter. However, before approaching this comparison—and in order to be able to eventually make it—it is necessary to wonder what the word *contemplation* means.

In *The World at a Glance* Edward Casey reminds us that the English language provides us with two terms that designate the two fundamental kinds of visual perception—namely, *gaze* and *glance*. Since there is no such distinction in French, to name these two types of visual perception one needs to match the general word *look* (*regard*) respectively with the adjectives *fixed* or *rapid*. Casey then explains that these two kinds of perception shall not be considered as specific and distinct acts, but rather as two "families," each of which includes multiple members that are more or less strictly related to one another.³ In the *gaze* family—that of the prolonged and attentive look—Casey includes precisely *contemplation*, which he characterizes as a "mode" of looking "open and patient—even to the point of being meditative."⁴ In other words, "I am *with* what I contemplate," just "as the 'con-' of 'contemplative' signifies."⁵ By welcoming the suggestion posited by the aforementioned Benjamin passage, I could add that, when one contemplates, one shifts in an *indistinction of activity and passivity* that constitutes precisely the other side of the *being with* what one contemplates.

It will then be important to wonder what kind of painting the spectator sees on the canvas that conveys him to contemplate. It is very unlikely that it will be a modern painting picture. Indeed, in the canvas evoked by Benjamin, nothing—no shock—should disturb the spectator's chance to "give himself up to his train of associations." Only a painting composed according to a way of seeing the world that has already been sedimenting in the tradition can hence offer such a possibility.

As is well known, the way of seeing the world that is still considered as dominant in the Western tradition is the one that was first formulated by the Italian architect and art theoretician Leon Battista Alberti in his 1435 treatise titled *De pictura*: "First I trace as large a quadrangle as I wish, with right angles, on the surface to be painted; in this place it [the rectangular quadrangle] certainly functions for me as *an open window through which the historia is observed*."⁶

Here Alberti explains a specific pictorial technique known by various names, amid which that of *linear* perspective, that is to say, the technique in which all the straight lines that are perpendicular to the plane of the painting converge toward a single vanishing point. For centuries—conventionally, we could say till the end of the nineteenth century—this technique has been considered as the fundamental law of Western painting. In order to confirm this, one only needs to recall that eighty years after the *De pictura*, in 1525, the German painter and engraver Albrecht Dürer contributed to the spreading of the technique theorized by Alberti by publishing another treatise titled *Underweysung der Messung mit dem Zirkel und Richtscheyt* (*Instructions for Measuring with Compass and Ruler*).⁷ This treatise contains a number of engravings—and more, which he will add in the second edition of the book, in 1538—representing the way in which the painter can draw in linear perspective by using a special device known as "Dürer's window." About the questions that concern us here, I would like to remark that one of these engravings particularly highlights the separation and opposition of the rigid posture of the artist with respect to the body of the model, which appears convoluted with desire.

However, Alberti's formulation was so successful that it has not simply characterized a certain way of conceiving the painting. More generally, this formulation echoes "the old metaphor of the eye as a 'window to the soul.'"[8] and, as I mentioned in the last pages of the previous chapter, turned it into the "*model*"[9] of a certain way of seeing, according to which we look at the world as through an open window. This *through*—namely, the prefix *per-* of the Latin word *perspective*—is precisely the term on which Panofsky will insist, despite some philological perplexities, when commenting the Albertian formulation.[10]

Starting with Alberti, the window hence becomes the "apparatus [*dispositif*]" undertaken by the epoch we call "modern" as the model of our way of seeing the world.[11] As highlighted by Marc Richir,[12] it is true that Descartes, in the second of his *Meditations on First Philosophy* (1641), rather tends to describe himself as *looking away* from the window, like Rembrandt's *Philosopher in Meditation* (1632). However, Descartes himself writes that "solely by the faculty of judgment which rests in my mind, I comprehend that which I believed I saw with my eyes"[13] when looking precisely through the window. Hence, we could say that the Cartesian judgment of the mind is but a reduplication of the vision through the window.[14]

According to Richir, Husserl's attitude is ultimately pretty similar: "To him, the world is a *picture* that is cut within the frame of the window."[15]

In short, in the so-called "modern" epoch, philosophy rejoins painting so as to assume precisely such an "apparatus" as the model of our way of seeing the world.

Figure 4.1. Albrecht Dürer, Draughtsman Making a Perspective Drawing of a Reclining Woman, 1538.

Figure 4.2. Rembrandt van Rijn, *The Philosopher in Meditation*, 1632.

Apparatuses and Historicities

On such basis, the "apparatus" shall not simply be understood as a *technical system*, or, to say it with Benjamin, as an *Apparatur*.[16] Rather, it should be understood, with Foucault, first of all as a "system of relations [*réseau*]"[17] which, as he explains apropos of the notion of sexuality, "allows diverse phenomena to be grouped together, despite the apparently loose connections between them [. . .]: behaviors, but also sensations, images, desires, instincts, passions."[18] In his turn, Gilles Deleuze remarks that the apparatus hence understood has an intrinsic connection not only with utterance, but also with visibility. The following passage by Deleuze is particularly rich in resonances with everything we are discussing here: indeed, to him apparatuses (*dispositifs*) are "machines that make one see and talk. Visibility does not refer to a general light that would illuminate preexisting objects; it is made up of lines of light that form variable figures inseparable from an apparatus. Each apparatus has its regimen of light, the way it falls, softens and spreads, distributing the visible and the invisible, generating or eliminating an object, which cannot exist without it [. . .]. If there is a historicity of apparatuses, it is the historicity of regimes of light but also of regimes of utterances."[19]

The thesis affirming the historicity of apparatuses is one and the same with the thesis concerning the historicity of the "environment," of the *milieu*, that these apparatuses contribute to elaborating, which Benjamin had clearly formulated in *The Work of Art*, where he names "medium" this kind of environment, and where he points out that "[t]he way in which human perception is organized—the medium in which it occurs—is conditioned not only by nature but by history."[20]

This thesis allows Benjamin to make explicit what he had affirmed in the previous sentence, which claimed the historicity of our way of perceiving the world: "*Just as the entire mode of existence of human collectives changes over long historical periods, so does their mode of perception.*"[21]

Usually, Benjamin's commentators only mildly remark that, a little farther on, he connects the historicity of our perception and of the environment "in which it occurs" (also thanks to the action of certain apparatuses) to another historicity, which he evokes by using a term referring to the semantic area of desire: "*the desire of the present-day masses to 'get closer' to things, and their equally passionate concern for overcoming each thing's uniqueness by assimilating it as a reproduction.*"[22]

As I said, usually the historicity of desire is not highlighted as much as the other forms of historicity I mentioned, nor is, of course, its intrinsic link with them. This is why I find it particularly important to enhance this point—even if it were only to criticize the fact that in the 1970s, in France, the dispute of poststructuralism against phenomenology affirmed the primacy of desire rather than perception—we saw it in the precedent chapter—as if the one could be produced without the other. On the contrary, for Benjamin, perception only modifies with desire and with its medium, and vice versa. In turn, such a historicity of desire cannot but rejoin what we have seen Deleuze claim apropos of the historicity of the "regimes of light," that is to say, that of the reciprocal references between the visible and the invisible. In other words, *the historicity of desire is one and the same with the historicity of visibility*, namely, the very visibility that our epoch restlessly seeks for, hence, on the one hand, proclaiming an improbable ideology of "absolute" transparency,[23] and, on the other hand, triggering a sort of iconoclastic countermovement,[24] both bringing along evident (and unsetting) implications in terms of relationships of power.

I would like to link this group of elements with a conception posited, once more, by Gilles Deleuze, according to whom "[w]e live with a particular image of thought, that is to say, before we begin to think, we have a vague idea of what it means to think, its means and ends."[25]

For Deleuze, this means that the operation of thinking is conditioned by the image of such an operation, which is transmitted to us by the culture we inhabit. However, on the basis of what we just said, isn't this also true as far as the operation of seeing is concerned? In other words, if, according to Deleuze, we have a preliminary image of thought that historically conditions our way of thinking, couldn't we add that we also have a certain image of vision—*an image of the way in which we see*—that conditions our way of seeing? This is one of the ideas that will emerge from my assessment, which means to suggest not only that the act of seeing has changed, in the human history, just as well as the *desire of seeing*. Indeed, my assessment also suggests that different images of seeing have been affirming themselves in different epochs of the Western history, and that each epoch has had the tendency to choose a particular optical apparatus as the model of the way in which, according to that particular epoch, we see. In other words, each epoch has conceived the way in which human beings see the world according to the characteristics of the optical apparatus that that very epoch ended up choosing as a model: this is what modernity did precisely with the window.

Evidently, this does not exclude that some of the characteristics of a particular optical apparatus can be transmitted from one epoch to the other. This seems to be the case with the quadrangular shape attributed by Alberti to the window, which he designated as the model of the pictorial representation based on the canons of the linear perspective. It is barely the case of highlighting that such a shape—i.e., the quadrangular, and more precisely, the rectangular shape—is still attributed to our images (and hence to their devices of production and reproduction) in such a dominant proportion that we take it for granted, while it is actually a most precise "cultural construct."[26] It is clear that this cultural construct refers to that of the linear perspective of the Renaissance, according to which a pictorial surface is conceived as the perpendicular section of the visual pyramid of the spectator, as a *veil* intersecting this pyramid, to say it, once more, with Alberti.[27]

In his by now classic book titled *The Language of New Media*, Lev Manovich also remarks this element of continuity linking the computer's screen, the cinematic screen, and the Albertian window: "Another feature of cinematic perception which persists [. . .] is a rectangular framing of represented reality. Cinema itself inherited this framing from Western painting. Since the Renaissance, the frame acted as a window onto a larger space which was assumed to extend beyond the frame. This space was cut by the frame's rectangle into two parts: 'onscreen space,' the part which is inside the frame, and the part which is outside. In the famous formulation of Leon-Battista Alberti, the frame acted as a window onto the world."[28]

Yet, Manovich does not try to dig any farther in searching for precedents. Indeed, he considers these three cases as examples of as many phases of "A Screen's Genealogy," which is for him "an intriguing phenomenon" typical of the "visual culture of the modern period."[29] I believe, however, that we cannot stop here. Let us try to go farther back in our history.

By referring to the Latin formulation of the aforementioned Albertian passage, the French art historian Daniel Arasse translates as "contemplate" (*contempler*) the term *contueatur*, which corresponds to the "*is observed*" of the quoted English version. He then remarks: "I have always been fascinated by the word *contemplate*. It has an extreme logic, for within *contemplate* there is *temple*. And the *templum* that was contemplated was the *square* or the *rectangle* that the Roman haruspex used to draw with their staff in the sky to wait and see how the eagles would cross it. According to the direction, to the number of eagles, and to their speed, the haruspex could interpret in a way or another what those signs said."[30] On this basis, Arasse highlights that a notion historically returns: that of "the delimitation of an area, starting in the sky, which then gets on the ground as *templum*, site of the sacred, and then again in painting as the Albertian quadrangle that institutes the *templum* of painting where the composition is contemplated."[31] In other words, the linguistic link Arasse sees is important in order to highlight a continuity between the haruspex's gesture and that of Alberti, both consisting in "delimiting" the surface of a "quadrangle" that our culture does not cease to invest with peculiar characteristics and with a particular relationship to our gaze. Indeed, "When put on the surface of the painting that is delimited by rectangular edges, paint as matter—what one squeezes out of paint tubes—becomes something else: that is, signifier, an object of art, of admiration, of interrogation. Paint is not just paint. The human adds something to it. Imaginary and symbolic are added to the real. When the painter puts his brush imbued with paint on the canvas, he leaves, in a sense, signs to be divined."[32]

However, by no means do these considerations seem to lead to *oppose* the pictorial canvas and the cinematographic screen, as Benjamin, on the contrary, had claimed by writing that only the first "invites the viewer to contemplation [*Kontemplation*]." Indeed, also the screen—and not just the cinematographic screen—appears as a quadrangular surface invested with peculiar characteristics and of a special relationship to our gaze, in which seems to survive some traces of what Arasse links to the Roman haruspex's gesture. These characteristics and this relationship to our gaze are such as to attribute to what appears on that surface a value *exceeding* its mere appearance. In short, to echo a sentence I mentioned above, we could say that what appears on the screen is not simply what appears. However, it is important to point out, as suggested by Georges Didi-Huberman apropos of the notion of "aura," that screens solicit the spectator to perform a contemplation that is *declined in a different way* with respect to that which the pictorial canvas invites him to enact.[33] Such a contemplation won't be of a kind that can be irremediably interrupted by, say, a visual shock; in such a contemplation, the element of "cult" will operate in a different way; its prefix *con-* will hence at once promise and menace an unprecedented immersion, as we will see in the next chapter. Therefore, a contemplation will still be possible. However, if I said that contemplation is situated in the indistinction of activity and passivity, this peculiar contemplation will be in an increasingly precarious balance between the first, which solicits our attention, and the latter, which catches us being troubled by the gaze as *objet a* of the screens that proliferate around us.

It must be added, however, that the custom of investing a certain surface with a privileged relation with truth seems to be much more ancient than the *templum* institution itself. First of all, this custom extends as far back as what the ancient Greeks called ἕδρα. Indeed, in his *Agamemnon*, first performed in 458 BCE, Aeschylus uses precisely this term, meaning a place devoted to the sacred contemplation of birds; that is to say, something similar to what Arasse describes above as *templum*.[34] Moreover, the aforementioned custom can even be traced as far back as the τέμενος, the "sacred enclosure," whose name significantly derives from the verb τέμνω, "to cut," and seems to be at the origin of the word *templum* as well.[35] However, if one looks deeper, the custom of conferring on a certain surface a privileged relationship to truth can also be found in the curtain that, in the sixth century BCE, Pythagoras inherits from the sacerdotal tradition to separate those having the right to see him from those who are only allowed to listen to him.[36] In this case, however, that surface does not *overdetermine* the visible as the *templum* does, but *forbids* it. Or rather, we could say that it *overdetermines* the visible by forbidding it.

How far back can one go in tracking what seem to be other examples of Lyotard's "*specular wall* in general"? According to Merleau-Ponty, one could go as far back as seventeen thousand years. Indeed, in *Eye and Mind* he writes, "From Lascaux to our time, pure or impure, figurative or not, painting celebrates no other enigma but that of visibility."[37] Merleau-Ponty, however, could not know the astonishing rupestrian images of the Chauvet Cave, discovered in France in 1994, which are thought to be "14.000 years older than those of Lascaux,"[38] and hence amid Europe's most ancient rupestrian pictures. When referring to them, it is hard to talk simply about "painting" or generally about "visibility." The choice to work on the darkest parts of the cave rather than the brightest; the game of lights produced by the torches that are necessary to admire those parts and to project on them shadow movements; the scrapes of some surfaces as a means to whiten them before all further interventions; the elaboration of kinetic figures; the three-dimensional effect that is often impressed on them by exploiting the conformation of the walls and by working on them with pictorial interventions or engravings; the sound accompaniment realized by beating the rocks and exploiting the echo effects: all these elements contribute to suggesting, more specifically, that what happened in the Chauvet Cave was a *sophisticated collective effort to contemplate moving images*, so much as to induce Werner Herzog to describe it as "almost like a form of proto-cinema,"[39] while Marc Azéma refers to it as "a real 'prehistory' of cinema."[40] Of course, such an effort aims to celebrate, generally speaking, what Merleau-Ponty called "the enigma of visibility," but I would say, more precisely, that it aims *to celebrate the enigma of images themselves, as well as the enigma of the surface that is invested with such a celebration and therefore delimited from the surrounding space.* That is, precisely the surface that Lyotard calls "the *specular wall* in general." By extending the language that Bernard Stiegler borrows from Derrida in speaking of "arche-cinema,"[41] I would propose to define such a "specular wall in general" as "arche-screen," understood as a transhistorical whole gathering the fundamental conditions of the possibility of "showing" (*monstration*) and concealing images on whatever surface. In our culture such a whole has been opened and experienced through the human body itself. In fact, the body can produce images simply by being interposed between a luminous source and a wall (as it happens in the myth of the origin of painting narrated by Pliny the Elder)[42] or by being decorated with inscriptions, drawings, colors, or tattoos. Besides, such conditions of the possibility of showing and concealing were developed in different historical ways by the rupestrian wall, or even by the simple wall itself, by the tent, the mirror, the veil (from the veil in the Biblical tabernacle, to Alberti's "intersecting veil," and onward),[43] but also by the curtain, the *templum*, and the window, as well as, later on, by the precinematic and cinematic screens, and even by today's computer screens. This list, however, is by no means exhaustive. In any case, our prehistoric and historic relations with these multiple surfaces imply connected variations in our respective ways of perceiving, desiring, and thinking.

In other words, I conceive the notion of arche-screen as a "theme" that—as I explained elsewhere[44]—does not give itself preliminarily to and independently from its "variations," which would platonistically depend on it and descent from it. Rather, the arche-screen should be understood as a sort of (musical) *theme* constituting itself *simultaneously with* its own variations and yet *exceeding* these very variations—since it is irreducible to them, but at the same time is inseparable from them and can only become by means of their own becoming. In this sense, the arche-screen exceeds the specificity of the various optical apparatuses and/or of the supports of vision that have historically produced its variations, even if they remain a decisive component in each of these variations.

In order to try to explore at least some of the conditions of the possibility of showing and concealing that are implicit in the notion of arche-screen, once we have traced the historically existent Chauvet Cave, we shall now necessarily turn to the mythical cave Plato conceived in *The Republic*, Book VI.[45]

Plato's Arche-Screen

In his "Allegory of the Cave," Plato talks about what is often translated as the "opposite wall" (τὸ καταντικρύ),[46] which works like a screen meant as a surface for showing images, since it is precisely on this surface that the Cave's prisoners see shadows of the objects carried by men behind them. Plato alludes just twice to this wall. The second time he imagines that it echoes the human voices sounding into the Cave, as if they came directly from the shadows.[47] It is the only allusion to a way in which this wall could indirectly contribute to *producing* rather than simply *reproducing* the illusion of images that are supposed to be "sensible reality" itself.[48]

The wall we are speaking of is opposed to another one, which Plato calls a *teikhíon*, a word meaning a low wall built along a road.[49] The Cave's *teikhíon* has the purpose of concealing the people carrying the various objects that rise above the low wall—similar to what usually happens with puppeteers. In fact, according to Plato's account, the *teikhíon* works as a *paráphragma*—a word often meaning a protective structure like a parapet or a bulwark[50]—from behind which the puppeteers exhibit the puppets to the audience.[51] Indeed, the word *paráphragma* (mainly used in the plural form *paraphrágmata*) has the same root as the verb *phrássō*, whose general meaning is "(to) *fence in*, (to) *hedge round*, hence with collateral notion of defence, *secure, fortify*."[52] Thus, the meaning of the word *paráphragma* in Plato's passage turns out to be very close to the original meaning of the word *screen*—to which Manovich, curiously, does not make any allusion in the aforementioned "A Screen's Genealogy," and which, starting at the end of the thirteenth century, comes to designate something giving shelter, protection, or concealment.[53]

Therefore, the *teikhíon* can be reasonably considered a screen as well, in the sense that it *protects*—according to the meaning of the Latin *pro-tegĕre*, that is, to "cover in front"—and hence conceals the men who are part of the machinery of the Cave, whose shadows, for this very reason, are not to be cast on the *opposite wall*. Moreover, from this argument one may infer that the *teikhíon* holds a selective task: indeed, the *teikhíon* picks out what has to be displayed on the *opposite wall* and screens off what, instead, has to remain hidden to the prisoners' eyes. Thus, in Plato's Cave the *opposite wall* (τὸ καταντικρύ) does not seem to be the only screen to take note of. Of course, insofar as it is the space on which the shadows are projected, it is easier to recognize its role at first glance. However, a closer reading may reveal that the *teikhíon* performs the double function of concealing by offering a protection and of selecting things to be shown—which are both, actually, characteristic of an "arche-screen." Lastly, consulting the Greek text, one might note that the comparison with the *paraphrágmata* undoubtedly recalls the meaning of the Old Frankish verb *skirmjan*, in which the word *screen* finds its original root.

Hence, I would like to state that in his "Allegory of the Cave" Plato presents the two fundamental possibilities of the arche-screen, that is, the screen as a concealing surface and the screen as a showing surface, neither of which can be merely opposed or separated from the other, either logically or historically. Besides, this is true also for the *figure* of the shadow itself, which the two screens described by Plato contribute to displaying. Indeed, the figure of the shadow is based precisely on the impossibility of dissociating a body presenting itself as a "negative screen"—namely, a surface that conceals, in this case, the light source, hence *producing* the shadow—from its complementary surface, which works as a "positive screen," namely, a surface that shows or *presents* the shadow.

However, besides this phenomenon, which in any case has a foundational role, a "negative screen" and a "positive screen," even if considered autonomously from one another, are portions delimited from the surrounding space, thus founding a peculiar relationship with it as well as the very *possibility of a third pole*. In the case of vision, this relationship is usually characterized as a *mutual* relationship between foreground and background. Indeed, as the *Gestalt* theory has pointed out, such a relationship *reciprocally* constitutes *the one as the visible of the other*, and it also founds a *point of view* as its third pole. In this sense, the arche-screen can be seen as a constituting part of the *fold* that allows vision itself. In fact, this fold produces the simultaneous blossoming of the visible foreground, its invisible background, and the viewer.

Both as a concealing and as a showing surface, the arche-screen *overdetermines* the space to which it is related. Thus, in one way or another, an arche-screen presents more than itself, it presents by *exceeding* itself. In this sense, it turns out that the arche-screen cannot be but an *excessive screen*, which, for this reason, cannot but solicit our desire in various forms, promising us "always 'something else to see,'"[54] as Merleau-Ponty puts it. This brings us back to Lyotard's question concerning the reasons for which "the *specular wall* in general [. . .] can become a privileged place of the libidinal *cathexis*" cited in the first part of the present book, for have we not found the answer right here? Of course, the arche-screen can mark the excessive feature of the concerned space in different ways: not only by simply *delimiting* but also by *superimposing* itself to that very space, or even by a combination of these two processes. In the first case, the delimited space is overdetermined in a *positive* way; whereas in the second case, the space is overdetermined in a *negative* way, since we are *forbidden* to see it. Actually, a prohibition is always a way to establish a communication with what is prohibited, and therefore *a way to exceed the prohibition itself*, as negative theology taught us on the one hand, and as "negation" does, on the other hand, in Freud's concept of the unconscious: "You ask who this person in the dream can be. It's *not* my mother," the patient says. Freud hence emends: "So it *is* his mother."[55] The screen as a way of presenting something negatively is also found in the aforementioned case of Pythagoras's curtain, and in another variation founding the theme of the arche-screen in our culture: that is, the case of the veil of Isis,[56] which precisely for its negative aspect was considered by Kant to be an example of sublime expression. As Kant himself writes: "Perhaps nothing more sublime has ever been said, or any thought more sublimely expressed, than in the inscription over the temple of Isis (Mother Nature): 'I am all that is, that was, and that will be, and my veil no mortal has removed.'"[57]

As is well known, one of the classical sources concerning that inscription is Plutarch's *De Iside et Osiride*,[58] according to which the veil of Isis is "variegated in color (for her essential power concerns the material, which becomes everything and receives everything . . .)."[59] As Plutarch points out, this veil is able to show Mother Nature's very nature—an always becoming nature, like that of images—precisely because *it has never been lifted.*[60]

Thus, Plutarch provides us with a variation on the motif that Merleau-Ponty would thematize nineteen centuries later with regard to a similar case when he will describe, in the wake of Proust, how we get to know what, in the first part of the present book, we heard him name "sensible ideas," that is to say, the essences of certain experiences, which only similar experiences can, sometimes, fully manifest, but cannot be *defined* by any concept. It is precisely apropos of such peculiar dynamics of our knowledge that Merleau-Ponty states that "here [. . .] there is no vision without the screen,"[61] meaning, as suggested in turn by Plutarch, that the screen is what allows vision. Nevertheless, the screen evoked by Merleau-Ponty has to be understood, in my opinion, as the "arche-screen" itself, rather than a particular case of it. Indeed, when one looks deeper, in the following sentence, Merleau-Ponty refers precisely to a sort of "arche-screenic" feature of our experience: "[T]he ideas we are speaking of would not be better known to us *if we had no body and no sensibility*; it is then that they would be inaccessible to us."[62] *The arche-screenic feature of our experience*, which emerges from this passage, *turns out being one and the same with our body* experienced as a space that is (inter)posed in the sensible to which it belongs. In this sense, the sensible itself—as well as its excessive feature—can be intercepted and hence be known.[63] Indeed, as we saw, *the arche-screen as such* shows us, either in a positive or in a negative way, the excessive feature of the space to which it is related, thus founding for us a positive or a negative presentation of the mutual references between this space and the world. In this sense, we can state—and I will return to this point—not only that *there is no vision without the arche-screen*, but also that *the arche-screen is, by its excessive feature, a surface instituting relationships*.

In this way, the arche-screen *accentuates* the *side* of our sensible relationship with the world called "imagination."[64] As I pointed out, this side does not simply concern vision; still, we may take vision as an exemplary case. If, as I stated, there is no vision without the arche-screen, then the arche-screen not only allows the direct power of vision but also releases that indirect or negative power of vision that is constitutive (but not exclusive) of imagination. This is what happens in the Italian poet Giacomo Leopardi's poem "L'infinito" ("The Infinite"),[65] in which he describes the sight of a "hedgerow" ("*siepe*") on a lonely hill. The term *hedgerow* reminds us of the verb "to hedge round," defining the general meaning of the Greek verb *phrássō*, which is close to the original meaning of the word *screen*. This hedgerow prevents the poet's gaze ("*guardo*") from seeing the view that stretches down the hillside. Nevertheless, when he sits and *contemplates* ("*mirando*")[66] the hedgerow, he is able to imagine "[u]nending spaces, / and superhuman silences, and depthless calm."[67] Thus, Leopardi's poem suggests not only that there is no vision without the arche-screen but also that there is no vision without imagination. In fact, if the arche-screen *allows* the former, it indeed *urges* the latter.

Moreover, we should point out that the inseparability of vision and arche-screen cannot but vary according to the different *prehistoric and historic variations founding the theme of the arche-screen in human culture*.[68] I believe we could ascribe to each arche-screen variation what Merleau-Ponty writes in *Eye and Mind* about the imaginary, which he describes as the actual's "pulp and carnal obverse exposed to view for the first time."[69] In other words, what appears in each variation of the arche-screen is expected to exceed what appears in fact, and therefore it is supposed to maintain a special relation with truth, leaving us with the suggestion that the arche-screen itself is a place devoted to these kinds of relations and therefore a place for the sacred, however it is taken.

Concerning the latter point, let me remind you that in the *Critique of the Power of Judgment*, Kant cites as a typically sublime example of *negative presentation* the Jewish commandment: "Thou shalt not make unto thyself any graven image" (*Exodus* XX: 4).[70] On the other hand, St. Paul's suggestion to move *per visibilia ad invisibilia* ("through the visible to the invisible") sounds more like a typical Catholic way of thinking about the sensible as a *positive although indirect presentation* of an exceeding super-sensible.

In his turn, Friedrich Nietzsche implicitly evokes Plutarch's view when, in 1886, he writes: "We no longer believe that truth remains truth when one pulls off the veil; we have lived too much to believe this. Today we consider it a matter of decency not to wish to see everything naked, to be present everywhere, to understand and 'know' everything [. . .]. Perhaps truth is a woman who has grounds for not showing her grounds?"[71]

Despite Plutarch's echo, Nietzsche indicates here his epoch as the one in which the idea of an inseparability between truth and its veil inaugurates the beginning of a radically new way of conceiving both truth and the veil. Following Nietzsche's suggestion, one might even be tempted to connect it with the by then imminent birth of cinema, understood as an optical apparatus that seems to be based on such an idea. Indeed, we already remarked all this in the first part of the present book, when we heard Merleau-Ponty evoke "a new idea of light" that was one and the same with a new idea of truth and of the screen, which I then related precisely to the emergence of cinema. Having said this, however, one should still resist the temptation of conceiving, once again, screens as a merely modern phenomenon. On closer inspection, we have discovered that human culture has constantly been haunted by the search for variations of an "arche-screen" in order *to see images*. Indeed, also in this sense, "to see is as a matter of principle to see farther than one sees."[72] Hence, even if "the screen" were to disappear, as many claim it will,[73] I firmly believe that the "arche-screen" would not.

The Invention of the Window and the Invention of the Subject

Let us get back to the variation of the arche-screen that coincides with the Albertian window, and let us raise once more the question that concerns it: What are the implications of assuming the window as the model of our way of seeing the world? The first implication is the division of space into two parts, which will be situated respectively on *this side* of the window and *beyond* the window itself. In other words, as I said in the beginning of the present chapter, these two spaces *face* one another. In this sense, the window itself attributes *opposed* features to these two parts, and—as long as the window is open or *at least transparent*—it attributes the role of *seer* to whoever occupies *this side* of the space it delimits, and the role of *seen* to whoever (or whatever) is placed beyond it. Assuming the window as the model of our way of seeing the world hence means conceiving vision as an operation characterized by the *separation* of the spectator from the show, by the *opening* or the *transparence* of what separates them, by their mutual *frontality*, and by the *opposition* of their features. Such an opposition is that of the seer and the seen, that is to say, of what is "here"—i.e., a "private area"—and what is "there"—namely, a "public area."[74] As a consequence, such an opposition implies that the *seer* is by definition *unseen*, and suggests—to refer to another traditional opposition that I will mention again later—that the *seer* is in the *shadow*, and the *seen* is in the *light*.[75]

Such an image of vision accompanies what Deleuze would call a certain "image of thought," namely, the dominant image of modern thought, whose fundamental features have been outlined between the fifteenth and eighteenth centuries and whose reckoned father is Descartes. Just as the image of vision taking the window as its model, such an image of thought places the world on the one side, by describing the world itself as a show and by defining it as an "object" that "faces" us—which is what the etymology of the Latin word *obiectum* means. In this configuration, we are placed on the opposite side, described as the spectators, and defined as "subjects." For indeed, insofar as we are separated from the show, we can elaborate a "representation" of it and we can possibly "support" its value of truth precisely because we are "placed underneath" it, as the etymology of the word *subject* suggests.

In short, we can say about the window thus understood what Giorgio Agamben, another contemporary thinker who referred to Foucault's reflection on apparatuses, wrote about them: "Apparatuses must always imply a process of subjectification, that is to say, they must produce their subject."[76]

To say this more generally and in phenomenological terms, if consciousness is always consciousness-of-something, its intrinsically relational feature can only imply a historicity that is at least as intrinsic. Consequently, consciousness, understood (precisely in a phenomenological way) as bodily consciousness, finds in each epoch its own historical shape within the bosom of our relationship to the perceptual and expressive environments that assure its connections with the world and with the others.

Gérard Wajcman confirms this by referring to the case we are examining here: "The invention of the window may have to do with the invention of subjectivity, given how it outlines respectively the territories of the world and of the self."[77]

Such a case hence indicates the intimate interpenetration of a reference optical apparatus, a given image of vision, a certain image of thought, and a particular "process of individuation that effects groups or people"[78] to use a Deleuzian expression, borrowed from Simondon, which—differently from *subjectification*, which Agamben takes from Foucault—has the virtue of not implying once more the reference to the term *subject*, thus avoiding to characterize it univocally and overhistorically, as suggested by Wajcman. I will discuss this further in the last pages of the present book.

In short, what we are examining here shows that the way according to which we believe we see influences the ways in which we believe we think and are in the world—and vice versa.

The Screen Rather Than the Window

In the light of these considerations, I would like to put the following question: What is the reference optical apparatus of our epoch?

Of course, it is true that the "image of seeing" that is still dominant in our way of speaking is still that of the window; it is also true that the cinema is also often thought of in the light of such an image,[79] and that to such an image refers even the world's most popular PC operative system ("Windows"). However, I think that *the screen as it affirmed itself beginning with the emergence of cinema* is what has become today's reference optical apparatus.

We shall remark that, like Benjamin, Alfred Hitchcock, in *Rear Window* (USA, 1954), also proposes to compare the cinema with the optical apparatus of the window so as to show, in turn, that the *essence of the cinema*—which he considers to consist in montage[80]—eludes the structure of the window. Indeed, the film's main character, Jeffries, who sits immobilized by his window in a pose that seems to allude to that of the spectator in the cinema hall, ends up being so implicated in the "show," that its main element—Thorwald, that is, the murderer he is about to unmask—to begin with, *sees him*, and then *irrupts in the private and dark area of his "here,"* hence abolishing it as a *separate* domain, so that the spectator peeping through the window ends up being literally *defenestrated*.[81]

By differentiating itself from the window, the screen has thus more or less consciously founded our present image of vision. This is why I think it has become, in our experience—but also, and increasingly, in our language—the point of intersection of the triple link that I evoked at the end of the first part of the present book. Consequently, I am convinced that understanding our relationships to screens today may help us understand our present experience of seeing, as well as the way in which our desire is changing. Also, I think that such an attitude toward screens comes from the attitude that the cinema has taught us, despite the multiple differences nowadays separating the two.[82]

Indeed, it has to be recalled that, in spite of these differences, the cinema is precisely what redistributed the relationships between darkness and light, opacity and transparency, space and spectator, by introducing a number of novelties that ended up slowly inscribing or consolidating in the meaning of the three words, sharing the same root, that designate the screen's surface in French, English, and Italian. In fact, I already had the opportunity to mention that "screen" (similarly to the French word *escrime*, i.e., fencing) derives from the Frankish verb *skīrmjan*, which means "to defend," "to protect by fighting." Hence, at least starting with the end of the thirteenth century, the word we are examining begins to indicate precisely an "interposed object dissimulating what it protects."[83]

On this subject, it is important to remark that the Italian poet Dante Alighieri, in the *Vita nuova* ("The New Life"), probably written between 1292 and 1293, uses this term to elaborate a metaphor that "is certainly optical," as recalled by Giorgio Agamben.[84] Such a connotation—which, indeed, does not cease to participate in the term's semantic evolution—will crucially consolidate its centrality in the beginning of the nineteenth century. It is in fact to the year 1810 that the *Oxford English Dictionary* dates the very first occurrence of the word *screen* in reference to a "phantasmagoria," that is to say, a rear projection of moving pictures produced by a developed version of a magic lantern precisely on a semitransparent screen. In his "Elements of Screenology,"

Erkki Huhtamo highlights that such an occurrence "represents a shift from the domestic sphere of furniture and personal accessories to the world of public entertainment."[85] It has to be added that such a shift reinforces and makes explicit the peculiar ambiguity that the French, English, and Italian terms designating the screen surface acquired in their use, that is to say, *the ambiguity of concealing and showing.*[86] Indeed, shifted "to the world of public entertainment,"*on the one hand*—a hand that is not only semantic, but also and primarily spatial—the screen keeps its characteristic of "protecting surface," meaning that it conceals from the gazes of the spectators the magic lantern, namely, the images' source of light and therefore the machinery producing them. *On the other hand*, that screen can "show" us the effects of such a machinery in a way that is all the more spectacular. Besides, Huhtamo notices that such an ambiguity was at work also in certain screen practices such as that of the shadow theatre, which we evoked, in a peculiar version, when considering Plato's Allegory of the Cave. Huhtamo recalls that the most typical form of shadow theatre was "introduced in Europe in the late 17th century," and played precisely with the ambiguity I just described. Indeed, "the audience sits in front of the screen, while the performers operate the shadow puppets behind it, between the screen and the light source. The spectators are normally allowed to see the moving shadows on the screen, not the 'machinery' animating them."[87]

It is with respect to the aforementioned case of phantasmagoria—extended in the so-called "cinema of origins," as we will see in the next chapter—that I feel it is important to highlight how the further developments of the cinematic apparatus will mark a progressive semantic shift of the word *screen* as referred to that apparatus. Indeed, *the ambiguity so far traced will tend to vanish* in this acceptance of that word, for the surface that such a term designates will cease to "protect" the source of light of the displayed images from one's gazes. In other words, the surface designated by the term *screen* will cease to separate a space on one side of it from a space beyond it, the latter being supposed to preserve metaphysically the secret truth of the first. It is primarily in this sense that I claimed that our present experience of screens is the outcome of what cinema has taught us.

On these bases, let us deepen the comparison between the Albertian window and the cinematic screen *understood as two models of vision*. As we know, the former separates and opposes a space situated on one side of the window from the other situated beyond it. We also know that the possibility of crossing with one's gaze the surface separating these two spaces—a possibility implied in the Latin word *perspectiva*, meaning "seeing through"—is conditioned by the convention establishing the virtual "opening" or transparency of the surface itself. In its turn, this surface needs to be adequately illuminated for the spectator's gaze. As for the cinema, it aims at obtaining an effect of transparency of the screen surface by exploiting the *indissoluble complementarity of light and shade*, not only in the images it produces, as painting does too, but also *in the relationship it establishes between the opacity of the screen, the luminous beam running into it, and the darkness of the cinema hall*. Thus, this screen *reflects*—i.e., literally "turns backward"—the luminous beam's light. As such, it provides its contribution to the work of *the cinematic apparatus*, which *inaugurates a space that does not institute any metaphysical "beyond," but makes visible a mythical "elsewhere."* I am writing precisely *elsewhere*: neither *beyond* nor *through*. Concerning this latter term, which takes us back to the perspectival model of the Albertian window, of course Benjamin is right when, in the passage I quoted at the beginning of the present chapter, he notices the difference between the images presented by the pictorial canvas and those presented by the cinematic screen. In the feature that is proper to the latter—i.e., the feature of movement—are rooted the progressive shifts of seeing, of the desire of seeing, and of the conception of seeing, which, in my opinion, the cinematic apparatus has gradually produced. As a child, when I saw western movies, I did not think that the Far West was *beyond* the screen, nor did I think that I was overlooking it as *through* a window. Rather, cinema *inaugurated* the Far West as an *other spatiotemporal dimension of my life* that would invite me to further appointments: in some TV series, for instance; but most of all such a spatiotemporal dimension would in fact wait for me whenever I would *create it anew* in my childish games. This is why it was an *other* dimension situated "everywhere and nowhere," and this is why I name it "mythical." Indeed, it then felt and still feels like it exceeded all distinctions between the imaginary and the real.

In this sense the cinematic screen shows us in a peculiar way that images are not at all "a tracing [*décalque*], a copy, a second thing"[88] that would depend on and descend from a *first* thing qualified precisely as "real."

But this is not enough: if the different prehistorical and historical variations of the "arche-screen" have always *solicited* and *oriented* the desire of those contemplating them, it is important to also highlight at least the complexity of the dynamics that keep intertwining in such a desire.

Just to recall some of these dynamics, we can affirm that Western culture has been dominated and is still marked by the desire of seeing *beyond* the screen surfaces (which, as we know, is thematized also precisely in the meaning of the word *metaphysics*). Besides, the modern developments of such a dynamic—which we can resume by "the desire to see the Truth"[89] of Nature and hence to "raise the veil of Isis"[90]—have intertwined with the tendency to see *through*, which has found its codification in the model of the Albertian window and in the Latin term *perspectiva*. The emergence of the cinema, for its part, seems to have rather intensified and made explicit another dynamic of desire. As such, this dynamic has always been at work as the desire of seeing "according to or with" the screen[91] in the sense I proposed in the first part of the present book.[92] Cinema has enhanced it to the point of making us dream of *entering* the screen itself. In the next chapter, I will linger on the changes that the "new media" seem to make in such a process and in the intertwining of this very process with others.

What it is possible to immediately highlight is that, if the window prepared for the *frontality of representation*, the cinematic and postcinematic screen increasingly prepares for the *enveloping of vision*, which of course has to be understood in a fundamentally *audiovisual* sense, and, in a near future, also in an increasingly *tactile* sense. In this perspective, the reason why in a sense the screen can be considered like a mirror—as we saw in Lyotard—is that it is, when looking deeper, a constitutive element of this folding of the visible on itself that we call vision.

Consequently, taking and intertwining the reflections of Walter Benjamin (historicity of perception and, simultaneously, of desire), those of Merleau-Ponty (ontological mutation at work in our epoch), those of Lyotard (mutation of desire at work in the Western societies beginning with the later nineteenth century), those of Foucault and Simondon (historicity of the apparatuses and of the processes of "subjectivation" or "individuation"), and those of Deleuze (historicity of a certain "image of thought"), we may then connect the twentieth century—understood as the century of cinema—to a progressive affirmation of an "image" of our encounter with the world detaching from the traditional frontality of the *theatrical* apparatus,[93] which serves as an inspiration to the window apparatus too.[94]

Indeed, our present experience of screens can no longer be reduced to that of the cinema. First of all, it has been modified by the television, whose luminescent screen "can present an event in the very moment in which it happens," while that of the cinema reflects the projection of recorded images.[95] Moreover, technology has focused its efforts on the cinematic screen so as to make us feel like dwarfs facing increasingly large images. Thus, in *A King in New York* (UK, 1957), Charlie Chaplin, who plays the spectator of a western film projected by means of the then-recent technology of the Cinemascope, in order to embrace by his gaze the huge images of a shooting taking place before his eyes, is obliged to feverishly turn his head right and left, as if he were attending a tennis match.

On the other hand, the TV screen, for its part, has got us used to feeling like giants facing lilliputian images.[96] When remembering that Plato, in his *Republic*, condemned images in general as they produced illusory effects by intervening on the "irrational" (*alogistikón*) part of our soul,[97] one is legitimated in wondering which effects might have been produced by the reverted dimensions of the images and ourselves and, at the same time, by the abandonment of the dark theater. In other words, it seems legitimate to question how these two simultaneous elements could operate on our system of values, on our myths and our desires. Roland Barthes's response would be: by detaching us from a hypnotic and erotic fascination, only to leave us "doomed [. . .] to the Family,"[98] as he wrote in reference to a certain phase of the televisual experience in the West. In this sense, my hypothesis is that such a detachment operated by the television with respect to the cinema delivered us to a *domesticated* erotism, as such compatible with the dimension of the "Family" evoked by Barthes.

However, the TV screen experience is far too important and far too complex not to be referred to an autonomous reflection.

More recently, the digital revolution has produced an apparently inexhaustible evolution and proliferation of the screens, which seem to be numberless. Our experience of the screens has hence ultimately become plural. At the same time, our experience of the screens is enriched by other novelties such as mobility, tactility, interactivity, connectivity, and a most peculiar "immersive character."[99] In the light of these features, the screens have become the *fundamental propulsive element* not only *of the transformations that are continuously at work in our relationship to images, but*, more generally, *of the perceptual, affective, and cognitive revolution* that affects us, even if, for the moment, we can only realize its most immediate consequences.

This is why I am convinced that questioning our present experiences of the screens will allow us to create a fundamental crosspoint for the philosophy we shall elaborate. In other words, we need to question such experiences in the effort to make a philosophy-cinema at today's scale—that is, a *philosophy-screens*.

5

Come Live with Me

The Seduction of the Screens Today

> The real ones want fictional lives and the fictional ones want real lives.
>
> —Woody Allen, *The Purple Rose of Cairo*

The Arche-Screen as a "Quasi-Subject"

The screen diverts, the screen captivates. The screen diverts and captivates *at once*. To say it with a single word, the screen *seduces*. In short, it takes us with it. Literally. To the point of inviting us *to live with it*.

This strategy of seduction, which is at once fascinating and troubling, has accompanied the cinema since its very origins. In 1902, Uncle Josh is so *affected* by it as a spectator that he gets to the point of ripping the screen down and to engage in a fight with the projectionist hidden behind it. Of course, in this way *Uncle Josh at the Moving Picture Show*—a film produced by the Edison Company and directed by Edwin S. Porter—shows that at the time the seduction of the screen was still connected to the reference to its *beyond*, which concealed its secret: the machinery. It also has to be remarked that this film echoes the famous anecdote—never historically proven—according to which on the occasion of the first projection of Louis Lumière's *L'arrivée d'un train en gare de La Ciotat* (*The Arrival of a Train at La Ciotat Station*), the spectators escaped from the movie hall, fearing that the wagon would run over them *by exiting the screen*. However, what is all the more important to highlight here is that the film produced by the Edison Company already shows a movie spectator who is so much *captivated* by the screen, he tries *to enter it*. This attempt and this temptation were destined to produce a most fundamental *topos* in the history of cinema and beyond. Actually, it seems to me that the cinematic experience of the screen finds a special expression in such a *topos*. Or, more subtly, what finds a special expression in such a *topos* is *the experience of the screen that the cinema at once promises and threatens* its spectators to live.[1] To linger over it for a little while would thus allow us not only to better understand such an experience of the screen; it would also allow us to estimate how this experience changes in electronic and digital media by observing the changes that these very media introduce in that *topos*.[2] In this way, we could specify both expectations and worries aroused by the peculiar *immersivity* of those media with respect to the kind of immersivity offered by the cinema.

Uncle Josh's temptation of entering the screen in the Edison movie will significantly become the little projectionist's *dream* in Buster Keaton's 1924 film *Sherlock Jr.*: a dream soon troubled by the continuous time-gap between the whirligig of situations on the screen and the actions by which the projectionist faces them.

Figure 5.1. Edwin S. Porter, *Uncle Josh at the Moving Picture Show*, 1902.

Later, this dream was nostalgically reversed as a daydream in Woody Allen's 1985 picture *The Purple Rose of Cairo*. Indeed, the male protagonist of this picture is a film character who, being in love with a spectator loving him in return, sometimes takes her into the screen, but most of the time escapes from his movie in order to live in the supposed-to-be reality, thus introducing comical effects of uncanniness in both situations.[3]

In any case, as I already mentioned, inviting the spectator to live on the screen seems to me like an element of seduction that is inseparable from the *film experience* as such,[4] and more generally from the experience of the specific film as it is *lived, realized, and re-elaborated* by the spectators themselves.[5] In my opinion, most of the technological improvements characterizing the history of cinema so far are as many attempts to feed such a seduction.[6] Evidently, this will be a seduction owing its efficacy first of all to the features of the film experience that we may qualify as "perceptual-affective," which will end up sedimenting in the spectator's own corporeity.[7]

The aforementioned notion of "film experience" was elaborated by Vivian Sobchack by making explicit reference to a characterization of the "aesthetic experience" that Mikel Dufrenne posited starting with his 1953 work focused precisely on the phenomenology of such an experience. Within it, Dufrenne aims at describing, first of all, the constitution of the "aesthetic object," which—he notes—gives itself as a primarily sensible object needing, in order to find its own accomplishment, the perception of a spectator. The correlation of the spectator and of his/her object—explains Dufrenne—has its originary stage in the "presence," where the corporeity of the first and the sensitivity of the latter compose a totality that is "not yet distinguishable."[8] Later, such an experience will be interrupted by the switch to "representation," but it will also possibly be reengaged and prolonged, albeit, of course, in conditions that will by then be different. The aesthetic object will hence be revealed to have a "world" proper to itself, with its peculiar sensible and affective structure. It is for this reason that Dufrenne defines it as a "quasi-subject,"[9] hence preluding, amid the rest, to the ontological rehabilitation of the sensible affirmed by Merleau-Ponty.[10] As for the aesthetic experience, for Dufrenne it may develop to the point of finding its climax in the sentiment, which will only arise by encountering the peculiar aesthetic object that is the work of art. Indeed, the work of art will manifest to the sentiment its expressivity, its affective world, hence developing, in its highest form, its own self-genesis of quasi-subject.

Vivian Sobchack borrows from Dufrenne precisely the notion of "quasi-subject," in order to characterize the configuration of film within the context of the movie spectator's experience.[11] Indeed, Sobchack highlights that the film gets to us "not merely as a visible object but also as a viewing subject."[12] At least, she points out, this happens "[a]t the level of our lived-experience of consciousness (rather than at the level of our thought)."[13] However, can we really distinguish and separate these two levels? Can we really *think* of a film by abstracting ourselves from the lived-experience we had of it? Indeed, if within such an experience the film is a "quasi-subject," will philosophy really be satisfied with thinking of it by means of concepts—be they elaborated by philosophy itself or by those whom Deleuze qualifies as "[t]he great cinema authors"[14]—hence making it become, once more, one of its study-objects? For my part, I tried to adopt the point of view of a "quasi-subject" when interpreting the experience of the screen as it is presented in *Uncle Josh at the Moving Picture Show*: namely, the point of view of the screen itself, as I highlighted in the first note to the present chapter. Indeed, if one can deal with the "aesthetic experience" or the "film experience," one can, no less legitimately, deal with the "screen experience," in whose horizon—and within whose horizon only—we can affirm that the screen configures itself as a "quasi-subject," as such bearing *its own perceptual and affective point of view*, as we have seen Žižek remark in the preceding chapter.[15] In turn, Manovich describes our relation to the screen in a way that not only does not neglect the fundamental perceptual-affective aspects of such a relationship, but also highlights, within it, certain characteristics of the "quasi-subject" that the screen can assume: "Rather than being a neutral medium of presenting information, the screen is aggressive. It functions to filter, to screen out, to take over, rendering nonexistent whatever is outside its frame. Of course, the degree of this filtering varies between cinema viewing and television viewing."[16] Still, "quasi-subject" characteristics are implicitly reckoned also by Sherry Turkle in the computer screen, when, on the basis of the experience we have of it, she describes it as "inanimate, yet interactive."[17] Such an interaction seems to be characterized first of all as a peculiar form of perceptual interrelation. In turn, a peculiar *perceptual* and *affective interrelation* is experienced manifestly—although not exclusively—in our relation to the images proposed by the screens (which are inseparable from them). Indeed, according to the perspective opened by the visual culture studies, within such a relationship images are to be considered—W. J. T. Mitchell explains it by words that significantly resonate with what we are discussing here—"as 'animated' beings, *quasi-agents*, mock persons."[18]

The elements I just evoked hence converge with a characterization of the screens understood as "quasi-subjects" first of all due to their being "aesthetic objects capable of expression," as we heard Dufrenne posit. As such, the screens produce a "quasi-agency"—an impersonal agency—by which they elude the traditional opposition that assigns to the subjects the feature of activity and to the objects the feature of passivity. It is hence with this peculiar status that they immediately inscribe in our sensible-affective correlation with the world, which is already crossed by a thinking that is, in turn, working on this side of the distinction of activity and passivity. Consequently, such a correlation will not cease to accompany, at least implicitly, both the representational distancing and the role of intellect and conceptuality in our relations to the screens.

Getting back to the first stage of this sensible-affective correlation, I shall point out that I would not qualify it as "presence" in the sense described by Dufrenne, but rather as "quasi-presence," since "imagination"[19] already slips into this experience a touch of what, in *Eye and Mind*, Merleau-Ponty calls "imminent visibility,"[20] which, as such, can only exceed all possible presence.

I am soon going to linger on such a feature of imminence. Meanwhile, I shall highlight that the so-far-outlined configuration of "quasi-subject" will not possibly be assumed in an exclusive way by a *certain kind* of screen or another. As a consequence, it should be considered as constitutive of what I proposed to name "arche-screen." Beware, however: I just said that the configuration of "quasi-subject" shall be thought of as *constitutive* of the "arche-screen." Now I would like to point out that, at the same time, such a configuration has to be thought of as *constituting itself differently* in virtue of its peculiar connotations—"whether discursive or nondiscursive," to say it with Foucault's formulation[21]—which it has been assuming during its prehistory and history. As a consequence, such connotations will inevitably go along with those of an experience that—also starting from the features related to our corporeity that in the preceding chapter I qualified as "arche-screenic"—*will* in turn *have constituted itself in the course of its prehistorical and historical variations*. In any case, it will manifest itself as an experience that we may define as *originally* "techno-aesthetic," to use a notion by which Gilbert Simondon aims at remarking that our *primitive* relation to the world has to be considered *already characterized from a technical point of view*.[22] Anyway, I shall return on this point in the next chapter. For the moment, it should be sufficient to recall the influence that Dufrenne had precisely on Simondon—an influence linked to some of their convergent exigencies—which in my opinion cannot be limited to the aesthetic domain alone,[23] but can also be traced in the very idea of attributing to the aesthetic objects a "mode of existence," hence ontologically rehabilitating them by the status of "quasi-subjects" having "a margin of freedom"[24]—a status assumed in the context of the constitutive correlation with humans that Simondon names "coupling."[25]

The Ambiguity of Seduction

It is hence in this sense and on these bases that at the beginning of the present chapter I spoke of seduction of the cinematic screen. However, when the cinema had to stage such a process of seduction, it could only revert to a series of actors playing—on the supposedly nonfictional screen of the cinema hall—the role of spectators entering the properly fictional screen shown in the movie. In other words, the cinema has always had to stage such a process of seduction by means of a *projection* of itself.

In order to account at least for a few of the transformations that took place apropos of this dynamic, we shall now examine a video displaying the relations that a giant interactive billboard installed in New York, in Times Square, by the fashion brand Forever 21 in June 2010, establishes with its spectators.

Designed by the interactive agency Space150, the screen features a model walking in front of a live image of the crowd below. The model occasionally leans over and appears to pluck someone out of the crowd. Sometimes she kisses them, and they turn into frogs. And sometimes, she drops them in her bag and happily trots off. At one point, the model takes a Polaroid snapshot of the crowd, shakes it out, and brandishes it in front of her—showing a zoomed-in image of the people below.

It seems to me that, generally speaking, the interactive screen experience is one of the most considerable present evolutions of our cinematic screen experience. Indeed, those screens significantly develop the *seductive attitude* characterizing the cinematic screen, which I am going to examine. More particularly, the billboard I evoked above on the one hand clearly shows a peculiar feature of urban screens and on the other hand gives us a most precious outlook on the way in which

Figure 5.2. The crowd in Times Square sees itself on Forever 21's interactive billboard, New York, 2010. Video still. © Digital Billboard by space150/Forever 21.

electronic and later digital media conceive not only their relations to their closest predecessors, namely photography and cinema, but also their relations to themselves, in both cases helping us to reflect on the transformations that have intervened in the screen experience that is at once proposed and promised to us.

Photography is indeed a predecessor that is explicitly evoked by the electronic billboard in question. In turn, cinema, which is the other predecessor I mentioned above, is rather implicitly evoked in many ways. Among these many ways, we find precisely the old promise, always on the edge of becoming a threat, which I anticipated above: namely, *allowing the spectator to live on the screen*. If the cinema always had to keep the promise by means of actors playing the role of the spectators, the aforementioned urban screen displays live images of *authentic* spectators, and it does this in two different ways. Firstly, the people walking about Times Square see themselves on the screen, and, secondly, in addition to this, some of them may discover they are the protagonists of a Polaroid snapshot taken by the model.

This essential difference in the way of making the spectator live on the screen is the outcome of two distinct ways of provoking the encounter between the spectator and the screen. Indeed, in the case of cinema, the spectator *choses* to encounter a screen, and, in order to do so, he/she goes *inside* a specific indoor space. Differently, in the case of urban screens like the one we are considering here, we may say that, in a way, *the screen itself is conceived and created in order to go meet the spectator*, hence producing an encounter that the spectator usually does not choose, and which is hence supposed to surprise him/her in the middle of an *outdoor* public space. Its seductive strategy hence appears to be much more explicit.

Besides, the giant billboard in Times Square confirms the typical dynamic—which I described in the preceding chapter—of the arche-screen, in whose virtue, as I already said, it functions as an element that is constitutive of the *folding* by which the visible institutes itself as such and simultaneously institutes a part of itself as viewer. Precisely as it produces the simultaneous and symmetrical development of the visible and the viewer, such a folding also allows their *reversibility*. Such reversibility appears for a moment in Buster Keaton's dream as a projectionist when, before entering the screen, he seems to be *stared at* by screen itself through the window between his cabin and the theater.

Actually, it is precisely in virtue of such a reversibility that the screens can promise (but also threaten) to make us live in their bosom.

Figure 5.3. Buster Keaton, *Sherlock Jr.*, 1924.

Hence, here a chiasm is gradually outlined: if, on the one hand, the correlation with the spectator constitutes the arche-screen as a "quasi-subject," on the other hand, and in return, the latter constitutes the spectator as a "quasi-image."[26] When one looks deeper, the terms of the question of immersivity are indeed there. Yet, why all these "quasi?" Because the reversibility we are dealing with is "always imminent and never realized in fact,"[27] as Merleau-Ponty wrote, or, according to his expression I quoted above, because what we are approaching here is an "imminent visibility." It is precisely thanks to this constitutive *imminence* that the screens can suggest the *uncanny promise* of making us live in their bosom, as I said, yet without being able to keep it. In other words, without ending up *con-fusing* the two poles—i.e., viewer and visible—of the reversibility which, by being fully realized, would inhibit vision itself. This is why no other word than "seduction" seems to express such a double-faced phenomenon in its *indivisible duplicity* of a promise destined not to be kept, a promise that hence sometimes tends to manifest a *double-faced* attitude. Precisely in this sense, the final bit of Woody Allen's *The Purple Rose of Cairo* is emblematic, for such a *duplicity* ends up, for once, being *split in two*. Indeed, the male film character is urged to return into the movie, and the *actor* interpreting him—despite his promise to remain with the lady spectator, to whom he had addressed love statements and proposals—goes back to Hollywood without her. All that is left to her, then, is to start dreaming again by sitting in the dark film hall.

As recalled by Sobchack, "three metaphors have dominated film theory's descriptions of cinema: the *picture frame*, the *window*, and the *mirror*."[28] My characterization of the arche-screen understood as an element constitutive of the folding of the visible onto itself—in other words, understood as the background *making us see* an image—distances us from the traditional representational models, which suggest we consider the screen as a sort of *frame* or *window*. Such a characterization shows, at the same time, that the *mirror*, in turn, is just a particular case of this folding of the visible in the viewer that institutes the vision. In fact, the mirror produces a reflexivity that is just a peculiar case of the reversibility I described above. Indeed, since the interactive screen we are dealing with shows live images of authentic spectators, we can state that it is a mirror much more than the cinematic screen has ever been. In this sense the interactive billboard also shows how contemporary mediality presents itself as a "sublation [*Aufhebung*]"—to borrow a Hegelian expression—of its predecessors.

As for the relations of electronic and digital media toward themselves, the images of the giant billboard in Times Square show that such media ostensively conceive the screen, rather than as a sort of window, as an optical apparatus that is most specific to them—and which dominates our epoch.

As I said above, I think that the progressive affirmation of what today we commonly refer to as *screen*, understood as the *autonomous apparatus* of our vision, already begins, in an inevitably contradictory way, with the "emergence of cinema" (that is to say, in the age that Frederic Jameson qualified as the "modernist" phase of capitalism, beginning with the 1890s),[29] and that it comes to an accomplishment in our postmodern age (beginning with the 1950s), in which, little by little, the screen becomes a *display*, a term univocally referring to the exhibition, exposition, ostentation of something. On this basis Francesco Casetti points out what follows: "The display shows, but only in the sense that it places at our disposition or makes accessible. It exhibits, but does not uncover."[30]

However, I would not assign to the display any kind of neutrality. On the contrary, I would also attribute to it, *mutatis mutandis*, what we heard Manovich affirm apropos of the cinematic screen and of the TV screen: it is "aggressive. It functions to filter, to screen out, to take over, rendering nonexistent whatever is outside its frame." Of course, sometimes the display is obliged to do this in a less explicit and frank way than its predecessors, but even in this case it remains somehow "aggressive," since *it does not cease to demand the gaze for itself* (even when it will be question of a "prosthesis of the gaze"),[31] and in this way it establishes a hierarchy in the visible, that is, it establishes a "regimen of light," like all apparatuses end up doing, as we heard Deleuze explain in the previous chapter. This is how the display ends up also claiming, in the name of what it exhibits, a peculiar *demand* for truth—no matter if and how it is founded—which, in turn, aliments the expectation of the gaze solicited at the same time by the display itself. Indeed, if the recognition of such a claim were not a precise *aim*, then why *exhibit* something, probably after laboriously manipulating it? Hence, the display—understood as a place producing this dynamic of exhibition and expectation of an alleged truth—reveals itself to hold a subterranean connection with the *templum*, providing, at the same time, an often mobile, temporary, and radically secularized version of such a place.

It is clear that the contemporary ideology of an "absolute" visibility, which I flagged in the previous chapter, is incarnated precisely by the display, hence understood. However, in the light of what we just observed, we shall affirm that the display, despite its name, cannot avoid "distributing the visible and the invisible," to recall once more Deleuze, hence ending up, I would add in Lyotard's words, "methodically disappointing" precisely the will to *realize* an absolute visibility.

In any case, the Forever 21 interactive billboard aims at celebrating precisely such a kind of display: namely, the very display that, in several videos, we see in the hands of the people in the crowd at Times Square, busy interacting with the billboard featuring their own image by filming it with their cameras, smartphones, and tablets. Still, in this way we find once more documented, and even enhanced, the *imminent reversibility* of the viewer and the visible that I described above, which the multiplication, giantification, or "Gulliverisation" of the displays make proliferate. Also, in this way, and in virtue of such an indelible imminence, the contemporary desire for "seeing everything" will end up, once more, being frustrated. In other words, it is not sufficient to graft cameras onto computer screens so as to "erase the crack that we considered to be constitutive of the visible order, namely that between *seeing* and *being seen*."[32] Otherwise, mirrors should have long since gotten there.

The Ambiguity of Desire

Giantification and "Gulliverisation" of displays: Erkki Huhtamo presents these two tendencies as being historically parallel and complementary in the production of "cult" effects.[33] Indeed, he points out that the miniaturization of visual supports does not erase the sacredness of images (which is, in my opinion, the heir of the ancient gesture of delimiting a space by assigning to it a privileged relation to truth). This miniaturization rather extends such a sacredness according to forms that are proper to it, by transposing it from the public to the private sphere. Nonetheless, Huhtamo admits that the tendency for shrinking gives us "an illusion of control"[34] over images, which their giantification seems, on the contrary, to make us lose, hence rather facilitating the immersion in the images themselves.

It thus seems legitimate to wonder whether the Gulliverisation of the screens implicates, amid others, the unaware search for a defense—at least partial, and precisely illusory—against their power of seduction, by means of the reduction of the risk of an all-encompassing immersion.

If this were the case, another ambiguity would correspond to the one that, as we have seen, is inherent to such a seduction, namely the ambiguity of the spectator's desire, who would want to *succumb to the seduction and at the same time resist it*, so as to eventually find the compromise indicated by Benjamin, namely, shorten distances.[35] The gesture of taking a selfie is emblematic: the distance is shortened to the length of an arm or, when one uses the special prosthesis named *selfie stick*, just a little more.

Besides, this latter example suggests that, in the postmodern condition of contemporary mediality, our screens-related desire is no longer that of *living in* the screen itself, but rather the one *of being present on screen-like surfaces at least for an instant*. Thus, the temporality of this desire is no longer that which, according to Deleuze, characterizes cinema, and which he defines, echoing Proust, as "'a little time in the pure state,' *and not in the present*."[36] In other words, Deleuze thinks that cinema would lead the spectator to live in the depth of a screen in which heterogeneous temporalities seem to be mythically co-entailed, thus composing a "time in the pure state." As Sobchack explains, electronic media—but the same could be said about digital media—rather invite people to "play and display"[37]—again, this term—in a *present* that I would consider just as *mythical*. Indeed, Deleuze characterizes the "mythical past" as "a past which was never present," that is to say, a "fragment" of "pure past."[38] In a similar way, we could define the aforementioned kind of present as "a present that is never present," since we never really live in its dimension.

In my opinion, such a mythical present is that very present evoked by the Superego of the postmodern condition, whose injunction is, according to Slavoj Žižek, "Enjoy *now!*"[39] It is a present turning upside down the contents of the Superego's traditional prohibition to enjoy. Precisely, that "now" is the untraceable—and therefore mythical—present of an enjoyment [*jouissance*] that is unachievable, since it is imposed by the Superego itself, that is, "[t]he cruel and sadistic agency that bombards us with impossible demands and then gleefully observes our failure to meet them."[40]

Besides, the expression *real time*, which has become omnipresent although it is completely meaningless outside of the field of informatics, seems to be another symptom of this very mythicization of the present. It is precisely this *mythical present* that electronic and digital media tend to conjugate with the *flat surface* of displays, thus showing a simultaneous mutation of the temporality and the spatiality of the related desire.

Despite what the Forever 21 billboard seductively shows, of course such a spatio-temporality "cannot be inhabited by any body that is not also an electronic body,"[41] as Sobchack puts it. Thus, here is the threat related to the seduction that these screens exert: in order to inhabit them, the human body has to be *reduced to its own mere surface*. In other words, such a requirement imposes aesthetic and ethical "demands" that, as we heard, Žižek characterizes as "impossible." A remarkable one is precisely that of Forever 21, meant as "be 21 forever!" The very insurmountable impossibility to satisfy this injunction seems to condemn all those whom the models pick out of the crowd to be turned into frogs or shut in a handbag by one of those fickle incarnations of the postmodern Superego.

Let us return to Times Square in order to watch another video that went viral on the Web: the one of a young man showing himself hacking screens in order to broadcast on them a video of himself explaining precisely that very hacking technique. Whether this hacking technique is a fake or not, this video allows me not only to confirm, but also to specify the terms of the modified spatiotemporality of desire at work in our present relation to the screens. That is: *to be present on their surface at least for an instant*, as I mentioned before, *in order to be able to see ourselves as others being seen by others*.

Such a dynamic—which reconfigures the relation between intimacy and extimacy in the light of the postmodern Superego and implies a

Figure 5.4. BITcrash44, "how to hack video screens on times square," YouTube, 2011.

redefinition of narcissism[42]—is doubtlessly at work in online social networks such as Facebook. We might even say that these kind of social networks owe their enormous success precisely to such a dynamic.[43] Nonetheless, we have to be careful: the "new expressivity" that social networks produce "is not simply narcissistic."[44] It is rather true that an element that can be thus characterized is an essential component of the desire that digital social networks have decisively contributed to spreading, namely, "the desire of individualization and expressive singularization, which makes each person's identity increasingly depend on the signs of acknowledgement received from others."[45] In this sense, such social networks have decisively contributed also to "magnifying"—meant both as "praising" and as "highlighting as never before"—the function of the screens understood as *surfaces instituting relations*. Of course, we are talking about relations that are presently marked by the dynamic I tried to outline apropos of the last video I analyzed. However, if this is true, it has to be reckoned that the success of digital social networks flags a surge of such dynamic, which—despite the death the myth assigns to Narcissus—urges us to look for an evidence, or at least a feedback, of our own daily existence in the relations instituted by the screens. Both the evidence and the feedback are of course idealized *for* and *by* the other's gaze, as it happens to the child in the Lacanian mirror phase—to which Lyotard also referred—by means of a parental gaze.

As a consequence, it would be restrictive to simply talk in terms of living *among* the screens today, for in fact we live *through* them. In this sense, there is no doubt that the "the culture of narcissism" at work in the postmodern condition[46] has found in the screens its most proper reflecting surface.

The video entitled *La Piège des images* ("The Trap of Images")—that the W Atjust agency realized for the French *Conseil Supérieur de l'Audiovisuel* in 2011—refers precisely to the desire at work in electronic and digital media. Here the dream of living in a screen is openly reversed in a nightmare. An anguishing atmosphere is suggested not only by the music, but also by images of toys abandoned in the rooms of a deserted house, as well as by the choked screams of a child hitting the various screens behind which he seems to be imprisoned.

This scenario prepares the appearance of the writing revealing the sense of what we have seen: namely, "Let us not allow our children to let images trap them!" In the credits screenshot, another exhortation follows: "Let us all feel responsible when facing the screens!"[47]

Figure 5.5. Mathieu Wothke, *La Piège des Images*, W Atjust, 2011.

What is striking about this video is the sensational contrast between the openly contemporary situation that is shown and the more than old-fashioned terms of the first exhortation. In it, one can immediately sense the echo of the condemnation of images established by that *simplified version* of Plato's philosophy named Platonism, which still accompanies our culture. However, this shall not make the novelty of the second exhortation go unnoticed. In fact, it explicitly indicates screens (in the plural) as the new means of contagion of the perennial danger of images. It looks as though the examined video takes the role of the vertical surface on which the shadows were projected in the Allegory of the Cave even more seriously than Plato himself did. This echo of such allegory may recall another echo, namely, that of *The Truman Show* (USA, 1998). Not only does this film reintroduce the nightmare of a self-centered environment in which images wield their absolute power of illusion and deceit. It also reintroduces the idea that from such a place escape is possible by reaching, beyond the wall surrounding it, the "exit."

As a consequence, the comparison between the last video examined above and the final scenes of this film suggests a decisive difference in the way the relationship with the respective screens is presented. Indeed, differently from the traditional film or television experiences, which were expected to remain *circumscribed* in space and time, the experiences of present screens, endlessly multiplying around and among us, threaten to make us unable to find, sooner or later, an exit.

Eventually, if our desire is changing in relation to the screens, it is also because their peculiar characteristics—which I listed at the end of the previous chapter—bring along a no less peculiar *awakening of ancestral fears*, such as that of remaining *imprisoned*. When one looks deeper, the nightmare of ending up defenestrated, as happens to the main character of *Rear Window*, is just a modern variant of these kinds of fears. However, it is a temporary and fictional variant, and in this sense it attenuates its own tragic feature, which indeed seems to be back today in its full radicalism. That of remaining *imprisoned* is hence once again a fear driven by the belief in a metaphysical separation, by means of a vertical surface, between an "inside" and an "outside."

Concerning this, it has to be observed that the creator of the TV show of which Truman finds himself the unaware protagonist is not wrong when warning him that "there is no more truth out there." Beware: the reason is not that reality—maybe due to the electronic and digital screens—has "disappeared," as someone claimed. Rather, it never existed as the first and last element, separated from the images through which we continuously face it. Reality and images shown by means of different apparatuses are and have always been in a mutual reference relationship. This is what Merleau-Ponty himself tried to suggest by describing vision in terms of *precession*.

6

Making Philosophy among and through the Screens

The New Prostheses

According to Francesco Casetti and Vivian Sobchack, the word *display*, more than any other, appears to be capable of defining what the screen is for us today. However, will it be enough in order to describe the experience of the screens that seems to be shaping in view of tomorrow? I would like to suggest that, concerning the future experience of the screens, it will be essential to also recur to another term, to which the perceptive revolution that is presently at work has assigned a new meaning, namely, the term *prosthesis*.

The reference to such a word is certainly not a novelty in the reflection on technology. However, I think that here it is important to evoke a few aspects of the *history* of such a word. The Greek term *próthesis* literally refers to an element facing or substituting another one. In virtue of such an etymology, in the medical domain—which is the point of departure of my reflection—a *prosthesis* is traditionally defined as whatever, organic or inorganic, serves to replace, completely or partially, a bodily organ whose functioning is somehow compromised, in line with "the classical paradigm of therapy or restoration."[1] However, this definition becomes restrictive, and hence problematic, when the shift of Western societies from an industrial to a "postindustrial" phase—namely, to what Lyotard named "the postmodern condition"[2]—goes hand in hand with a technological leap that proves to be huge, even from a qualitative point of view. Thus, the term *prosthesis* acquires a broader meaning with respect to its etymology, and is hence used to designate a number of "artefacts" that not only serve to *reestablish*, but also to *amplify* and even to *alter* the human possibilities of perceiving (understood as inseparable from movement), feeling, knowing, and acting. Indeed, scientific innovation has started intervening on the human body not only, as it used to happen, by means of electromechanical or chemical artifacts, but also via miniaturized technologies whose finality increasingly consists in improving human potentialities—in "extending" them, to say it with the term used by Marshall McLuhan.[3]

Of course, in the case of wearable technologies, what will be empowered is the relationship between the body wearing them and the world that surrounds it. Indeed, such technologies will make our aesthetic-sensible[4] relation with that world interact with the information about it that is simultaneously acquired, hence allowing us the encounter with an "augmented reality." For these reasons, wearable technologies mainly pivot on the spatial side of such an encounter—although it is evident that, space and time being inseparable in our experience, they will be alike in the reality that is augmented by these prostheses.

Besides, a very different kind of "prosthesis" is currently producing mutations that are just as deep and invest more directly the temporal side of our "being-in-the-world." Hidetaka Ishida, a Japanese scholar in Western philosophy, talks about it precisely in these terms,[5] but he is certainly not the only one to have traced such a dynamic. The American media theorist Richard Grusin has shown this process at work in the U.S. information media after the event of 9/11, but points out its tendency to become global. He defines it as *Premediation*[6] and describes it as the programmatic attention consecrated by these kinds of media to whatever potentially traumatic future event, in order to avoid producing effects of shock in our lives, like those that occurred in the aftermath of the Twin Towers attacks. As a consequence, Grusin affirms that "[p]remediation is [. . .] distinct from prediction. Unlike prediction, premediation is not about getting the future right. In fact it is precisely the proliferation of [. . .] future scenarios that enables premediation to prevent the experience of a traumatic future by generating and maintaining a low level of anxiety."[7]

I experienced this peculiar process myself, in late October 2012, when I arrived in New York a half-day before hurricane Sandy raged. Then, the local news invited the population to get food supplies and barricade themselves in their homes during the following two nights and days. Inevitably, one ended up spending most of that time watching those local news outlets, waiting for an information update, which, just as inevitably, hardly ever came. Hence, the journalists—who were sent to key places in town—provided live coverage of surreal facts, such as the special envoy at the south end of Manhattan, who, deeply focused on his scoop, showed that a certain step in a little staircase descending toward the bay had by then been submerged, while the previous day it was still dry!

In short, the possible imminent catastrophe had been *premediated* through what we may consider, properly speaking, as "non-news," which was broadcast "both to generate anxiety and to suppress it."[8]

This is how the aforementioned process is actually at work in the information media: rather than focusing on the present or on the recent past, they tend to mainly concentrate on the temporal dimension of the future, in order to limit the social concern related to such a dimension in a time of catastrophes, which seems to have been inaugurated as such by 9/11.

In turn, Ishida refers to another amid the most emblematic catastrophes of our time: the Japanese earthquake of 3/11/11, which provoked a tsunami and, consequently, the Fukushima nuclear disaster. Ishida explains that, already in those days, Japan disposed of a computer system capable of alerting the population, even via mobile phone, within a few seconds from the beginning of an earthquake, warning them at once of the possible related consequences. In my opinion, Ishida does not adequately take into account that such a system is connected, properly speaking, to an event that just happened, and is hence not imminent. Nonetheless, it has to be remarked that this system has, amid others, a function resembling the one that Grusin traced in the present information media: namely, that of limiting the anxiety that the risk of catastrophes spreads in society, by assuring that such risk is under control at all times. Concerning Japanese society, such a function is performed by what Ishida, in an explicit reference to Husserl, defines as "the cybernetic alarm circuit that *prosthetizes* the 'protension' of the *human* time,"[9] that is, what phenomenology would also call "lived time."

In short, the present information media analyzed by Grusin and the alarm system described by Ishida perform a similar function: namely, that of a *prosthesis* that can only be qualified as *temporal*. However, in this case we are not dealing with the aforementioned inorganic artifacts. Here, the mediatic or cybernetic component rather becomes the part of "a thoroughly heterogeneous ensemble consisting of discourses, institutions,"[10] knowledges, and powers, to say it with Foucault: in short, one of the "ensembles" that he proposed to name "apparatuses [*dispositifs*]." Still, these apparatuses, similarly to the inorganic artifacts, seem to function as "new prostheses" and, as such, they offer us, in turn, a *development of our potentialities* in exchange for a *delegation*. The latter word appropriately suggests an ambiguous relation between the delegating party and the delegate, rather than a radical alterity between the two. Without such a relationship, the first could not give the second—in a way that it considers as provisional and reversible—the mandate to act on its behalf. In the case we are studying here, what will be delegated is a tiny portion of our control over ourselves, which we would accept to give up by undergoing a moderated dose of what we heard Grusin name "anxiety," whenever we see the words *Breaking News* on the TV screen. In return, what will be enhanced is our capacity to face the future, which seems to be increasingly exposed to the risk of all kinds of catastrophes.

Besides, it has to be remarked that such a temporal prosthesis does not *superpose* to a "human time" that, thanks to it, would remain protected from the becoming of history. Rather, it tends to *converge* in human time itself, hence transforming it with respect to the becoming of history.

In short, once more the development of our potentialities projected by today's prostheses—no matter if their results are actually or supposedly real—directly and radically invests our aesthetic-sensible relation to the world, which clearly implies not only perception, but also memory, imagination, and desire.

Besides, it has to be added that, within such a relationship, the development of our potentialities also reveals to be the reverse of an *an-aesthesia*:[11] in our case, precisely that of "anxiety."

Not so differently from what McLuhan wrote about media understood as "The Extensions of Man," today's prostheses are hence characterized not only by the couple "development-of-potentialities/delegation," but also by the couple "development-of-potentialities/anaesthesia." As for the latter term of this second couple, it might be appropriately defined as the tendency "to reduce the exhibition of sensibility to contingency,"[12] by protecting in the first place what phenomenology literally considers as our horizon of tension toward the future.[13]

In conclusion, human sensibility—increased, delegated, anaesthetized—is subjected to such a deep mutation to the point that we can definitely understand this change's decisive scope, but surely not its long-term consequences.

The Screens and 9/11

The two examples of new prostheses that we have examined so far—indeed, two emblematic examples—have the screen as their interface of choice. In fact, it is the screens, in the first place, that produce the augmentation of reality that defines the experience of AR. As for the role they play within the temporal prosthesis we just considered, we only have to read a few more lines drawn from the writings I quoted apropos of this subject:

> ISHIDA: I myself, being at that very moment in Tokyo (about 375 km away from the epicenter) [. . .] immediately received a notification [. . .] on my mobile phone, whose *screen* showed the epicenter and the dimension of the earthquake and highlighted in red the tsunami alerts.[14]

> GRUSIN: The immediacy of the bombing, burning, and collapse of the Twin Towers coupled with the hypermediacy of its mediation on *screens* across the world [. . .] [and] led many to describe 9/11 as the "first live global media event."[15]

Hence, today the screens occupy a central position amid the new prostheses that are transforming our aesthetic-sensible relation to the world, given that they can work as prostheses by themselves, just as they can work as decisive components of furtherly elaborated prosthetic *apparatuses* (*dispositifs*). As we heard Grusin suggest, it has to be added that they were given a fundamental impulse in assuming such a position by the event of 9/11.[16] Of course, the "iconic turn"—which, on the wave of the digital revolution, has opened our lives to experiences capable of transforming our visual relation to the world—has been developing since the 1990s, and certainly, without it, 9/11 would not have been "the first live global media event." Moreover, the powerful impulse to make us *live among and through screens*, which such an event has performed, *was not* entirely actualized on that day. In fact, what made 9/11 become "the first live global media event," was primarily the most familiar of screens—namely, the TV screen. Still, this is not enough to rescale the impulse produced by 9/11 in the direction of making us live, more and more, among and through screens. Indeed, on that day, the groundbreaking novelties of the "iconic turn" were suddenly *put before the eyes of the whole world together with the attacks*. They merged with them in an eminently visual event, whose impact changed our way of looking at the world itself.[17] As if then such novelties had been exhibited in their huge potentiality—that of transforming "the whole world population into a benumbed witness"[18]—which, over the following years, the new media would majorly exploit, hence attempting on certain aspects of the primacy of television, and even undermining it amid certain portions of the audience.[19]

Apropos of this, I find that the first episode of the TV series *Black Mirror*—whose title aims at evoking the screen in its evolutions and proliferations today and in the near future[20]—is emblematic. The episode to which I am referring, titled *The National Anthem*, written by Charlie Brooker, directed by Otto Balthrust, and broadcast in the UK in 2011 by Channel 4, is based on a bizarre criminal project developed during the years following 9/11 in order to provoke once more a "live global media event." The young Princess Susannah—member of the British Royal Family, who at some point is acidly referred to as "princess bloody Facebook, bloody echo-conscious national sweetheart"—is mysteriously kidnapped—and death-threatened, in case the prime minister refuses to have sex with a female pig on a live TV broadcast. Despite being a surrealistic affront rather than a bloody terrorist attack, this event—first required and later obtained—features multiple direct and indirect references to 9/11. As for the indirect references, it is enough to mention that one of the points recalled in the TV news on the first anniversary of the humiliating live-broadcast sexual intercourse, is that "one art critic caused controversy by describing it as 'the first great artwork of the twenty-first century'" (a clear allusion to the puzzling declarations delivered by the German musician Karlheinz Stockhausen only a few days after the collapse of the Twin Towers). Another point evoked in the same TV news is the mention of the number of spectators that had watched the live event, which, on this basis, is defined as "an event in which we all participated."

By using such references, this episode hence seems to put the following question: Only a few years after 9/11, which exalted once more the primacy of television, what if other criminal minds conceived a way to provoke a "live global media event," and a Western government tried to prevent its broadcasting by putting pressure on the state television? The answer is: by that time, the primacy of television, which seemed to be incomparable, would be reduced due to the fact that a portion of the audience prefers new media, which are just as capable of giving a global reach to an event, even when a state television has to bow to the government's will of censuring. In short, the thesis suggested by the episode is that television seems to increasingly reduce to the last terminal (which, as a general knot, is still indispensable) of an information system that can still count on the aggressive concurrence of the Internet, and particularly YouTube, Twitter, Facebook, and so on.

All together, but also by their differences, the screens of all these media hence compose our *global agora*, which has inevitably also become our *global arena*. Therein, certain dynamics can be tragically displayed—from 9/11 to the beheadings performed by the Isis militants—and others circulate in concealment—I think in particular of those concerning so-called big data.[21]

Besides, nowadays television seems to be precisely the indispensable general knot I mentioned above, also within the temporal prosthesis apparatus described by Grusin. However, this is not its only role. Indeed, Allen Feldman makes reference once more to the event of 9/11, in order to give television a no less central role. More particularly, Feldman examines the sequence of images that, on the TV screen, is inevitably associated to those attacks, namely, the second plane crashing into the South Tower. "It was as if the audience was being given *temporal therapy* by witnessing a mechanical sequence of events, over and over, which restored the linearity of time, which had been suspended with the assaults,"[22] Feldman writes. Giving the audience such temporal therapy is precisely television's other crucial role.

In a time of catastrophes, television hence ends up working as a temporal prosthesis aiming at *restoring* and *developing* at once some of our abilities. Besides, with this characterization of our epoch as a time of catastrophes, the postmodern condition seems to lose its previous tendency to question mainly its ambiguous relation to modernity, considered as its own past, so as to rather face the challenge—precisely under the threat of catastrophes—of what seems to be its peculiar future. This is where begins its pro-ject of pro-tection of pro-tensions by means of pro-sthesis capable of premediating the time to come (à venir)—indeed, the importance of the preposition *pro-*, which indicates the orientation toward what is placed *before* (*devant*), speaks for itself.

Actually, I don't mean to claim that these therapeutic or prosthetic effects are an exclusive characteristic of the present time. Its distinctive mark is rather the link between such effects and its self-representation as a time of catastrophes, which, of course, was prepared by a modernity soaked in a sense of human finitude and in a belief in progress that ended up collapsing in Hiroshima, due to the climax of progress itself.[23] Still, therapeutic or prosthetic effects such as the ones I evoked so far seem to be discernible also in Walter Benjamin's interpretation of the Freudian psychoanalysis, by means of which he characterizes modernity as an "increasing atrophy of experience."[24] In fact, this interpretation is so close to Feldman's and Grusin's analysis (both of which indeed echo it), that it sounds as if it had also been elaborated in the aftermath of 9/11, and referred to it: "In Freud's view, consciousness as such receives no memory traces whatever, but has another important function: protection against stimuli [. . .]. The threat from these energies is one of shocks. The more readily consciousness registers these shocks, the less likely are they to have a traumatic effect."[25]

In the words by which Benjamin interprets Freud, hence, we can already find the exigency of social "protection" against the perceptual and emotional shocks that are typical of a certain epoch—in its case that qualified as "modern." We saw Grusin detect a similar exigency in our time. Moreover, we can find that Benjamin already remarked the implicit need to restore the control over one's own perceptual and emotional life, which is occasionally troubled by the experience of shock, even if such control will be achieved to the detriment of one's own lived memories. This is indeed the same therapeutic need that we heard Feldman formulate when referring to the "traumatic effect" of the shocks provoked by the images of 9/11.

As for the media's response to such needs, in "The Work of Art in the Age of its Technological Reproducibility," Benjamin emphasizes "the shock effect of film, which [. . .] seeks to induce *tightened* attention"[26] that, in turn, would precisely contribute to protecting the humans living in the newborn modern metropolis from similar effects. In the light of what I have been saying so far, Benjamin's reflection on this point hence ends up retrospectively revealing that screens *have always been*—at least since their introduction in the world of public entertainment—prostheses developing our system of perception-memory-imagination-desire. But this is not enough: by using Benjamin's own terms, it shall be remarked that *such prostheses reveal to be the reverse of an atrophy*. Beware: not in the sense that an atrophy imposes the use of a prosthesis, but rather in the sense that the prosthesis implies an atrophy. In other words: *technologically strengthening is what produces a certain atrophy.*[27]

This, hence, allows the emergence of the mutual connections between the couples of features characterizing the "new prostheses," which I highlighted at the end of the first paragraph of the present chapter. I am referring to the development-of-potentialities/delegation couple and to the development-of-potentialities/anaesthesia couple. In fact, we can now claim that such a development provokes a sort of callus or mithridatization—these seem to be the underpinned models of Benjamin's and Grusin's reasonings—which in turn produce addiction and hence an-aesthetization. That is, according to the Grusin passage I already quoted, "to prevent the experience of a traumatic future by generating and maintaining a low level of anxiety." At the same time, this development implies a delegation which, together with the an-aesthetization, contributes to atrophying, as least as a trend, the autonomous performance of the delegated ability.

Subjectification, Individuation, Dividuation

How about the aesthetics which, in the *Critique of Pure Reason*, Kant characterized as the reflection on space and time understood as *a priori* forms organizing our sensible experience? This is a crucial question, since we just acknowledged how far the "new prostheses" go in transforming our sensible experience; so far as to even modify the spatiotemporal forms themselves. Besides, this acknowledgment is enough to account for the critique addressed to the Kantian transcendental aesthetics by Husserl's phenomenology, which accuses it of not having explored the originary aesthetic-sensible experience to which subjectivity itself attributes the spatiotemporal forms, beginning with our body's relation to the world. However, Husserl tends to consider this subjectivity as "a universal, ultimately functioning subjectivity,"[28] and the experience I just evoked—the one founding the "Lifeworld" (*Lebenswelt*)—as an "invariant." Patočka's consequent reply is the following: "We do not even perceive in the same way as ancient Greeks even though, physiologically speaking, our sense organs are the same. Humans in a secularized epoch see not only different things but see them differently."[29]

In turn, Vivian Sobchack reminds us that, far from being an invariant, our own lifeworld is the world of screens.[30] Moreover, I would like to point out that the transformations in the aesthetic-sensible experience tend to be retrojected, by acting on the supposed *a priori* forms of such experience, which, hence, properly speaking, are not *a priori*, but rather highlight a *becoming transcendental of experience itself*. An example of this is provided precisely by the "new prostheses," since they can imply retroactive effects on the human abilities, which hence are no longer to be considered as established once and for all.

This is the reason why, instead of speaking of *subjectivity*, it would be more appropriate to speak of *subjectification*, a term that, in fact, Foucault used to designate the historical process of affirmation of a certain configuration of the subject, and, at the same time, of a certain apparatus (*dispositif*). However, this term ends up referring once more to the notion of "subject," with the risk of giving us an overhistorical characterization of it. This is why I think the best option would be to recur to a term posited by Gilbert Simondon, namely, *individuation*. On its basis the term *subject*, despite the use that Simondon himself made of it,[31] can be restricted to designating a specific and historically characterized form of individuation.

As we know, to the traditional concept of individual understood as the stable final product of a preliminary metaphysical process, Simondon opposes the idea of an individuation in metastable becoming, which can come to a halt in the physical stage, or get as far as the biological stage, or even proceed to the psychic and collective stages.

Here I would like to focus on these two latter forms of individuation, which are "reciprocal to one another."[32] In fact, I think that such notions efficiently describe our constitutive and precisely metastable relations with the affirmation (which will of course enhance the collective side of such relations) of certain power and knowledge apparatuses, but also with the "new prostheses" understood as "technical objects" that, as Simondon himself explains, can, in turn, cross several individuations in an indivisible coupling with our own individuations (whose psychic side will then stand out).

Besides, as I mentioned in the previous chapter, the foundational feature of such a coupling leads Simondon to believe that our aesthetic-sensible relation to the world is inseparable from a technical mediation, and hence pushes him to raise the need to elaborate what—in the draft of a 1982 letter to Jacques Derrida—he names a "techno-aesthetics."[33] Indeed, the term *techno-aesthetics* aims at naming our aesthetic-sensible relation to the world (with its own affective tone), understood as a primitive relationship that is already technically (and hence historically) characterized, as well as being an always renewed "scene of individuations" (*théâtre d'individuations*),³⁴ involving both us and the technical objects with which we are, as I already said, inseparably coupled.

It is against the background of such a conception that I would like to place a claim Giorgio Agamben posits after having broadened his interpretation of Foucault's apparatuses (*dispositifs*) so as to include therein also what we have so far named "new prostheses." Agamben writes: "The same individual [. . .] can be the place of multiple processes of subjectification [. . .]. The boundless growth of apparatuses in our time corresponds to the equally extreme proliferation in processes of subjectification."³⁵

In the light of Simondon's critique of the concept of individual, Agamben's remark seems to describe our coupling with the "new prostheses" as the scene of multiple individuations, and hence pushes us to approach certain problems raised by the wave of thought designated by the term *posthuman*, which aims at questioning the traditional conception of the human essence in its purity and stability. These are questions that we can see displayed in a moment of Spike Jonze's film *Her* (USA, 2013), whose action takes place precisely in the near future shaped by the digital revolution. I am referring to the moment in which the main character, who has a romance with his computer's operating system (featuring Scarlett Johansson's voice), asks "her" whether "she" has other affairs. Her digital-neat reply is: 641 users. However, after acknowledging the shock, the film, despite having raised the question, does no longer linger on it. Hence, it somehow admits—as the main character does explicitly—not to have an understanding of such question, and thus simply carries on by taking refuge in the reassuring conventions of the dramatic comedy. Still, these are decisive questions that emerge when raising a multiple and "migrant" characterization of *identities* understood as assigned, at each occurrence, *on the basis of the relationships* each one of us has with everyone else and with the world.³⁶ In fact, if my partner says, "I love you," not only to me, but, at the same time, to 641 other people, what about my identity, which I am used to considering as stable and unique? What about the identity that is so reassuring to consider as somewhere I can get back to despite my relations? What about the identity that defines me as an individual? Actually, the operating system's aforementioned reply allows us to glimpse precisely the explosion of my self-representation as an *individual*. Indeed, it shall not be forgotten that this latter word—which, as we know, is foundational of modernity—means, literally and blatantly, *indivisible*. On this basis, such a reply rather announces the uncanny discovery of a condition of *dividuality*.[37] In other terms, since at each occurrence "individuation" *becomes* the other side of one of the multiple relations that intertwine us, then it can only lose all implicit reference to an indivisible residual, and in this sense it has to rather be conceived as a *dividuation*. It seems to me that this latter word is capable of naming the condition to which refers what we heard Agamben qualify as the "boundless growth of [. . .] [the] processes of subjectification."

Indeed, my aim is not to affirm that the "boundless growth of apparatuses in our time" inaugurates such a condition, as Agamben seems to claim. I rather aim at suggesting that certain technological novelties interact once more with a certain ontological condition: they are made possible by it, they highlight it, and they re-elaborate it at once.[38]

Already a few years back, the American psychologist Sherry Turkle began to describe precisely such a re-elaboration: "The self is no longer simply playing different roles in different settings at different times, something that a person experiences when, for example, she wakes up as a lover, makes breakfast as a mother, and drives to work as a lawyer."[39]

By reading in the experience of computer games the symptom of a novelty that would later spread in the most differentiated relations toward screens as well as with the multitude of windows that screens themselves can simultaneously open, Turkle highlights that, differently from the condition she described before, in the present, "the life practice of windows is that of a decentered self that exists in many worlds and plays many roles *at the same time*."[40]

Living among and through screens urges us to think precisely of such a condition. Indeed, if the Albertian windows has been the emblem of Being understood as the universal opposition of subject and object, the windows appearing on the electronic and digital screens—by generating plural and virtually simultaneous interactions in a network—"have become a powerful metaphor for thinking about the self as a multiple, distributed system."[41]

Such a condition hence seems to extend, manifest, and re-elaborate Being understood as *becoming, multiplicity, and relation*, according to the ontological connection and the logical primacy that these features have in common.

Still, how *is it possible* to *think* of a Being thus conceived? Simondon warns us that the conceptual logic is not capable of doing it,[42] since the concepts are supposed to *de-fine* entities that are necessarily considered as stable and unitary—in short, substantialized—and not to display relations. In other words, the conceptual logic seems to refer to the Albertian window optical apparatus understood as model of our relation to the world: "a substantialized *individual* facing a stranger *world*," to say it, once more, with Simondon.[43]

Consequently, the conceptual logic cannot possibly comprehend the ontological and logical novelties implied in the screens apparatus.

We can remark that the critical and suspicious attitude Simondon professes as to the notion of concept, rejoins the attitude common to the philosophical reflection developed in France apropos of the cinema—of course, on the basis of different evaluations concerning it—from Bergson to Merleau-Ponty.[44] We would hence affirm that the critique of the notion of concept has pointed at a "philosophy-cinema" capable of taking into account the ontological and logical novelties implied by the screens apparatus. In other words, it has pointed at what I call "philosophy-screens." Indeed, the present proliferation of screens is one and the same with that of images and of their own logic.[45] It is the logic of our sensible relation with the world, in whose name aesthetics was founded. Such logic inevitably ends up exceeding and hence contesting that of concepts, to which it had been claimed to be reducible, in spite of all. However, in the gaps between the fingers of our hand, squeezing in the gesture of seizing—the gesture on which the modern action of conceptualizing was shaped—*we* increasingly *feel that sense* is slipping away. Without falling into a rhetoric of the ineffable, the philosophy to be made is called upon to account for this.

Notes

Acknowledgments

1. See Mauro Carbone, "Falling Man: The Time of Trauma, the Time of (Certain) Images," *Research in Phenomenology* 47 (2017): 190–203.

Chapter 1. Sartre and Deleuze via Bergson

1. Gilles Deleuze, "Nota dell'autore per l'edizione italiana," [1974, Italian trans. Armando Verdiglione], in *Logica del senso*, Italian trans. Mario de Stefanis (Milan: Feltrinelli 1975); English trans. Ames Hodges and Mike Taormina, ed. David Lapoujade, "Note to the Italian Edition of *The Logic of Sense*," in *Two Regimes of Madness* (New York: Semiotext(e), 2006), 66.
2. Gilles Deleuze, *Différence et Repetition* (Paris: P. U. F., 1968), trans. Paul Patton, *Difference and Repetition* (New York: Columbia University Press, 1994), XXI.
3. In the French educational system, *Khâgne* is a two-years-long program in Humanities that students attend after secondary school graduation in order to prepare for the competitive entrance examination to the Écoles Normales Supérieures. [T. N.]
4. Jean-Paul Sartre, "Apologie pour le cinéma. Défense et illustration d'un Art international," in *Écrits de jeunesse*, ed. Michel Contat, Michel Rybalka (Paris: Gallimard, 1990), 388–404.
5. Alain, *Propos sur l'esthétique* [1923] (Paris: P. U. F., 1948), 13.
6. Ibid., 15.
7. Ibid.
8. Ibid., 14.
9. Sartre, "Apologie pour le cinema," 388.
10. Ibid.
11. Ibid.

12. Ibid.
13. Ibid.
14. Ibid., 389.
15. Ibid.
16. Ibid. The three passages by Bergson, which Sartre quotes, are respectively taken from the *Essai sur les données immédiates de la conscience* (1889), from the second of the talks given in Oxford in 1911 and titled "La perception du changement"—which were later anthologized in *La Pensée et le Mouvant* [1934]—and from *L'énergie spirituelle* (1919).
17. Sartre, "Apologie pour le cinema," 390.
18. Ibid.
19. Ibid.
20. Gilles Deleuze, *Cinéma 1. L'image-mouvement* (Paris: Minuit, 1983), trans. Hugh Tomlinson and Barbara Habberjam, *Cinema 1. The Movement-Image* (Minneapolis: University of Minnesota Press, 1983), 1.
21. Ibid., 3.
22. Sartre, "Apologie pour le cinéma," in *Écrits de jeunesse*, 390.
23. See Ibid., 31–32.
24. Ibid., 26.
25. Deleuze, *Cinema 1*, 2.
26. Ibid., xiv.
27. Here, I am evoking the title of Jean Wahl's famous book *Vers le concret. Étude d'histoire de la philosophie contemporaine (William James, Whitehead, Gabriel Marcel)* (Paris: Vrin, 1932), which is notoriously used to characterize the typical philosophical attitude of the so-called three Hs generation (Hegel, Husserl, Heidegger), that is, the generation of Sartre and Merleau-Ponty, among others. On this subject, cf. Vincent Descombes, *Le même et l'autre. Quarante-cinq ans de philosophie française (1933–1978)* (Paris: Minuit, 1979).
28. "Not for one instant did he [Bergson] *look at* his images" Sartre writes in *Imagination* [1936] (Paris: P. U. F. 1962), trans. Kenneth Williford and David Rudrauf (London: Routledge, 2012), 59.
29. Deleuze, *Cinema 1*, 56.
30. Michel Contat, Michel Rybalka, "Notice" for Jean-Paul Sartre, "Apologie pour le cinéma," in *Écrits de jeunesse*, 385.
31. Deleuze, *Cinema 1*, 227, n. 18.
32. After describing the attitude of Husserlian phenomenology with respect to "things," Sartre writes: "One is perhaps reminded of Bergson and the first chapter of *Matter and Memory*. But Husserl is not a realist." Jean-Paul Sartre, "Une idée fondamentale de la phénoménologie de Husserl: l'intentionnalité" (1939), in *Situations I* (Paris: Gallimard, 1947), trans. Joseph P. Fell, "Intentionality: A Fundamental Idea of Husserl's Phenomenology," *Journal of the British Society for Phenomenology* 1, no 2.

(1970): 4–5, reprinted in *The Phenomenology Reader*, ed. Dermot Moran and Timothy Mooney (London and New York: Routledge, 2002), 382–84, here 382.

33. Deleuze, *Cinema 1*, 56–57.

34. Deleuze, *Cinema 1* and *Cinéma 2. L'image-temps* (Paris: Minuit, 1985), trans. Hugh Tomlinson and Robert Galeta, *Cinema 2. The Time-Image* (Minneapolis: University of Minnesota Press, 1989).

35. This tendency is particularly clear in the following passage from *Cinema 1*, which I shall quote at length: "Another path, however, seemed open to Bergson. For, if the ancient conception [of movement] corresponds closely to ancient philosophy, which aims to think the eternal, then the modern conception, modern science, calls upon *another* philosophy [. . .]. [T]his is a complete conversion of philosophy. It is what Bergson ultimately aims to do: to give modern science the metaphysic which corresponds to it, which it lacks as one half lacks the other. But can we stop once we have set out on this path? Can we deny that the arts must also go through this conversion or that the cinema is an essential factor in this, and that it has a role to play in the birth and formation of this new thought, this new way of thinking? This is why Bergson is no longer content merely to corroborate his first thesis on movement. Bergson's second thesis—although it stops half way—makes possible another way of looking at the cinema, a way in which it would no longer be just the perfected apparatus of the oldest illusion, but, on the contrary, the organ for perfecting the new reality." Deleuze, *Cinema 1*, 7–8.

36. Paola Marrati, *Gilles Deleuze. Cinéma et philosophie* (Paris: P. U. F., 2003), trans. Elisa Hartz, *Gilles Deleuze. Cinema and Philosophy* (Baltimore: The John Hopkins University Press, 2008), 95.

Chapter 2. The Philosopher and the Moviemaker

1. Pascale Fautrier, "Le cinéma de Sartre," in "Ce qui le cinéma fait à la littérature (et réciproquement)," *Fabula LHT (Littérature, histoire, théorie)* 2 (1er décembre 2006): § 3; http://www.fabula.org/lht/2/Fautrier.html.

2. François Albera, "Maurice Merleau-Ponty et le cinéma," *1895 Revue d'histoire du cinéma* 70 (été 2013): 121. Albera highlights "L'Herbier's effort not to limit his institution to the status of a professional school, but to rather make it become 'a cinema faculty.'" Ibid., 122.

3. This is Dudley Andrew's thesis: at the time of the Liberation, "Bazin was the obvious nomination for director of cultural services [at IDHEC] [. . .] Bazin gave lectures and arranged for films and speakers, such as Merleau-Ponty who lectured there in March 1945." Dudley Andrew, *André Bazin* (Oxford: Oxford University Press, 1978, Revised edition, 2013), 75. This thesis is not confirmed by François Albera's quoted article "Maurice Merleau-Ponty et le cinéma."

4. Maurice Merleau-Ponty, "Le cinéma et la nouvelle psychologie" (1947); trans. Hubert L. Dreyfus and Patricia Allen Dreyfus, "The Film and the New Psychology," in *Sens et non-sens* (Paris: Nagel, 1948), trans. Hubert L. Dreyfus and Patricia Allen Dreyfus, *Sense and Non-Sense* (Evanston: Northwestern University Press, 1964), 48–59.

5. Published for the first time in *L'écran français* 17 (24 octobre 1945): 3–4, then reproduced in Mauro Carbone, Anna Caterina Dalmasso, Elio Franzini, eds., *Merleau-Ponty e l'estetica oggi / Merleau-Ponty et l'esthetique aujourd'hui*, "Cahiers de *Chiasmi International*" (Milan-Paris: Mimesis, 2013), 21–24.

6. Ibid., 23.

7. Ibid., 24.

8. Maurice Merleau-Ponty, *Phénoménologie de la perception* (1945) (Paris: Gallimard, 1992); trans. Donald A. Landes, *Phenomenology of Perception* (New York: Routledge, 2012), XXXV.

9. On this subject, it is important to remind what Hugh Silverman explains on the basis of the notes taken by Fernand Jacquet—namely, an auditor attending Merleau-Ponty's lectures at the University of Lyon. As Silverman reports, in 1946–47 Merleau-Ponty gave, among others, a course ranging "from a consideration of contemporary aesthetics, and a discussion of Cézanne, cinema, cubism, Malraux, to the significance of the psychology of art. Much of Merleau-Ponty's interest in this material is reflected in the first part of *Sense and Non-Sense*." Hugh J. Silverman, "Translator's Preface," in Maurice Merleau-Ponty, *Consciousness and the Acquisition of Language* ("La Conscience et l'acquisition du langage," in M. *Merleau-Ponty à la Sorbonne, 1949–1952. Résumé de ses cours établi par des étudiants et approuvé par lui-même*, "Bulletin de psycologie," t. XVIII, n° 236, Paris: 1964, 226–259), trans. Hugh J. Silverman (Evanston: Northwestern University Press, 1973), xxxiii.

10. Merleau-Ponty, *Sense and Non-Sense*, 59.

11. Ibid., 27.

12. Ibid., 28; my emphasis.

13. Ibid., 50.

14. Ibid.

15. Ibid., 50–51.

16. Ibid. 52.

17. Ibid.

18. Ibid.

19. Ibid., 54.

20. Ibid.

21. Enzo Paci, "Introduzione," in Maurice Merleau-Ponty, *Senso e non senso*; Italian trans. Paolo Caruso (Milano: Il Saggiatore, 1962; later Milano: Garzanti, 1974), 13.

22. Merleau-Ponty, *Sense and Non-Sense*, 54.

23. Ibid.
24. Ibid.
25. See Pierre Rodrigo, "Merleau-Ponty. Du cinéma à la peinture: le 'vouloir-dire' et l'expression élémentaire" (2005), in *L'intentionnalité créatrice. Problèmes de phénoménologie et d'esthétique* (Paris: Vrin, 2009), 235–55.
26. Ibid., 250.
27. Ibid.
28. Ibid., 252.
29. Ibid., 253.
30. Ibid.
31. See Ibid.
32. Merleau-Ponty, *Sense and Non-Sense*, 54.
33. This is what Jean-Pierre Charcosset remarks in his *Merleau-Ponty. Approches phénoménologiques* (Paris: Hachette, 1981), 23.
34. Merleau-Ponty, *Sense and Non-Sense*, 48.
35. On this subject, see Jean-Paul Sartre, "Apologie pour le cinéma. Défense et illustration d'un Art international," in *Écrits de jeunesse*, 390: "One can [. . .] apply [to cinema] what Bergson elsewhere said about music."
36. Merleau-Ponty, *Sense and Non-Sense*, 49.
37. Ibid., 54; my emphasis.
38. Ibid.
39. Merleau-Ponty, *Phenomenology of Perception*, 223.
40. Marcel Proust, À *la recherche du temps perdu*, vol. I: "Du côté de chez Swann," ed. Pierre Clarac and André Ferré (Paris: Bibliothèque de la Pléiade, 1954); trans. Charles Kenneth and Scott Moncrieff, *Remembrance of Things Past*, vol. I: "Swann's Way" (London: Wordsworth Editions, 2006), 334.
41. Merleau-Ponty, *Sense and Non-Sense*, 49.
42. Ibid. (Translation modified, *T.N.*).
43. Henri Bergson, *L'évolution créatrice* (Paris: Alcan, 1907); trans. Arthur Mitchell, *Creative Evolution* (London: Macmillan, 1954), 322–23.
44. Merleau-Ponty, *Sense and Non-Sense*, 54.
45. Pierre Rodrigo, *L'intentionnalité créatrice*, 252.
46. Merleau-Ponty, *Sense and Non-Sense*, 54.
47. Ibid., 55.
48. Maurice Jaubert, the most important cinema musician in France before World War II, quoted by Merleau-Ponty in Ibid., 56.
49. Charcosset, *Merleau-Ponty. Approches phénoménologiques*, 22.
50. Merleau-Ponty, *Sense and Non-Sense*, 57.
51. Immanuel Kant, *Kritik der Urteilskraft* (Berlin u. Libau: Lagarde u. Friedrich, 1790); trans. Paul Guyer, Eric Matthews, ed. Paul Guyer, *Critique of the Power of Judgement* (Cambridge: Cambridge University Press, 2000), 192. On this subject, it is important to recall, on the one hand, that according to Kant

aesthetic ideas work in a "symbolic" way—that is, indirectly and analogically (§59, 225)—and, on the other hand, that in his "Apologie pour le cinéma," Sartre affirmed that "it is a *natural* symbolism, in its genesis" what is at work in the cinema's way of thinking (Sartre, "Apologie pour le cinema," in *Écrits de jeunesse*, 394). The possible Kantian echo of such a claim cannot be determined.

52. Merleau-Ponty, *Sense and Non-Sense*, 57.

53. For reasons of consistency with respect to Carbone's other books that have been published in English, and to the English translations of Merleau-Ponty's work, through the present book I will translate the French term *sensible*—meaning, on the one hand, "capable of sensations and perceptions," and, on the other hand, "capable of sentiments"—with the English word *sensible*, which therefore has to be understood according to the double meaning of the French term [*T.N.*].

54. Ibid., 57–58.

55. Ibid., 53–54.

56. Proust, "Swann's Way," 334; my emphasis.

57. Paul Klee, "Schöpferische Konfession," *Tribune der Kunst und Zeit* 13, ed. Kasimir von Edschmid (Berlin: Erich Reiss, 1920); trans. Norbert Guterman, "Creative Credo," in *Theories of Modern Art: A Source Book by Artists and Critics*, ed. Herschel B. Chipp (Berkeley: University of California Press, 1973), 182–86, here 182.

58. Merleau-Ponty, *Sense and Non-Sense*, 58.

59. Ibid.

60. Ibid., 49.

61. "This talk begins by addressing to students and scholars in film, to practicians, wishful practicians (the 'Louis Delluc' award), and probably to a few 'theorists' (like Moussinac, Sadoul, Mitry, Damas, who lecture in the Institution or are its fellows)." Albera, "Maurice Merleau-Ponty et le cinéma," 121.

62. Ibid., 59.

63. Christian Metz, *Essais sur la signification au cinéma* (Paris: Klincksieck, 1968); trans. Michael Taylor, *Film Language. A Semiotics of the Cinema* (New York: Oxford University Press, 1974), 42–43. I owe the recommendation of this passage to Anna Caterina Dalmasso, whom I take here the opportunity to thank.

64. Ibid.

65. Merleau-Ponty, *Sense and Non-Sense*, 58.

66. See Stefan Kristensen, "Maurice Merleau-Ponty, une esthétique du mouvement," in *Archives de philosophie* 69 (2006): 137, n 31.

67. Maurice Merleau-Ponty, Jean-Luc Godard (propos recueillis par), "Le testament de Balthazar," *Cahiers du cinéma* 177 (1966): 58–59.

68. Maurice Merleau-Ponty, *Notes de cours au Collège de France 1958–1959 et 1960–1961*, text established by Stéphanie Ménasé, "Préface" by Claude Lefort (Paris: Gallimard, 1996), 390–91.

69. Ibid., 391. The expression *fundamental thinking* indicates here precisely a sort of "spontaneous philosophy," of "thinking of the *Ungedachte*" (Ibid.), where a relation between man and Being is at work, which philosophical thinking has not yet properly *thought*.

70. Ibid., 391.

71. Ibid. The "painting-cinema" couple is evoked once more by Merleau-Ponty in the preparatory notes of the third course he consecrated to the "Concept of Nature," titled "Nature and Logos: The Human Body" (1959–60): "These relations of the visible and the invisible, of the logos of the visible world and of the logos of ideality, will be studied (*The Visible and the Invisible*) only in the next years with language, with other systems of expression (painting, cinema), with history and its architectonic." Maurice Merleau-Ponty, *La Nature. Notes. Cours du Collège de France*, ed. Dominique Séglard (Paris: Seuil, 1995); trans. Robert Vallier (Evanston: Northwestern University Press, 2003), 227.

72. Ibid., 391.

73. Ibid. For putting into perspective the combination of the birth of the cinema and the heritage of the philosophical reflection on movement, see Pierre Montebello, *Deleuze, philosophie et cinéma* (Paris: Vrin, 2008), 11–16.

74. Merleau-Ponty, *Notes de cours au Collège de France*, 166.

75. Maurice Merleau-Ponty, *Le Visible et l'invisible*, text established by Claude Lefort (Paris: Gallimard, 1964); trans. Alphonso Lingis, *The Visible and the Invisible* (Evanston: Northwestern University Press, 1968),157.

76. Maurice Merleau-Ponty, *L'œil et l'esprit* [1960–1961] (Paris: Gallimard 1964), trans. Michael B. Smith, "Eye and Mind," in *The Merleau-Ponty Aesthetics Reader*, ed. Galen A. Johnson (Evanston: Northwestern University Press, 1993), 144–45.

77. Maurice Merleau-Ponty, *Résumés de cours. Collège de France 1952–1960* (Paris: Gallimard, 1968); trans. John O'Neill, "Themes from the Lectures at the Collège de France, 1952–1960," in Maurice Merleau-Ponty, *In Praise of Philosophy and Other Essays* (Evanston: Northwestern University Press, 1988), 78.

78. Saint Aubert refers to such a transcription in his essay titled "Conscience et expression chez Merleau-Ponty," *Chiasmi* 10 (2008): 85–106. He points out that "[t]his document has a privileged position in the evolution of Merleau-Ponty's philosophical work. First of all, along with the *Recherches sur l'usage littéraire du langage* [*Studies on the Literary Use of Language*], it is the first course at the Collège de France: Merleau-Ponty put a remarkable attention in its preparation, whose length corresponds to approximately 130 pages of an ordinary edition. The date is also very important: we are in early 1953, that is, just after the thesis period, which ended in 1945, following the author's most existential phase (1945–1949), and after three years of courses at the Sorbonne (1950–1952). These last two periods witnessed the birth of the notion of flesh

and the emergence of the topic of expression, particularly in the unpublished preparation of the lectures given in Mexico City in early 1949, and, two years later, in the lecture on *L'homme et l'adversité* [*Man and Adversity*] and in the writing of the fundamental manuscript *La prose du Monde* [*The Prose of the World*]. By its very title, the course on *The Sensible World and the World of Expression* realizes the junction between the major theme of Merleau-Ponty's main thesis—i.e., perception—and that, which is hence more recent, of expression." Ibid., 85–86. See also Emmanuel de Saint Aubert, "Conscience et expression. Avant-propos," in Maurice Merleau-Ponty, *Le monde sensible et le monde de l'expression. Cours au Collège de France. Notes, 1953*, ed. Emmanuel de Saint Aubert, Stefan Kristensen (Geneva: MētisPresses, 2011), 7–38.

79. Kristensen refers to this transcription in his essay titled "Maurice Merleau-Ponty, une esthétique du mouvement," 123–46. Here he significantly announces that, by examining Merleau-Ponty's course notes, his essay aims at focusing "on the Merleau-Pontian phenomenology of movement, [and on its] relations to the cinema" so as to get to "Jean-Luc Gordard's relation to phenomenology and to indicate the premises of a dialogue concerning Deleuze's approach to the cinema." Ibid., 123.

80. Maurice Merleau-Ponty, "Themes from the Lectures at the Collège de France, 1952–1960," in *In Praise of Philosophy and Other Essays*, 73 [Trans. modified, *T.N.*].

81. Ibid.

82. See Merleau-Ponty, *Le monde sensible et le monde de l'expression. Course au Collège de France. Notes. 1953*, 66, 68, 93, 97.

83. Merleau-Ponty, *Phenomenology of Perception*, 283. See also Ibid., 287, where Merleau-Ponty writes, with reference to Wertheimer, "The psychologist leads us back to this phenomenal layer. We shall not say that it is irrational or anti-logical. This would only be the positing of a movement without a moving object."

84. See Merleau-Ponty, *Le monde sensible et le monde de l'expression*, 92, quoted by S. Kristensen: "Maurice Merleau-Ponty, Une esthétique du mouvement," 128. Here Kristensen reminds us that "there is in Bergson an implicit reference to the body, but due to the lack of 'a theory of the perceiving body,' he misses the problem of movement 'in the order of phenomena' and ends up assimilating the divisible duration of the worldly temporality to the duration proper to consciousness." Ibid.

85. Merleau-Ponty, *Le monde sensible et le monde de l'expression*, 102.

86. See Kristensen, "Maurice Merleau-Ponty, une esthétique du mouvement," 129. References to Merleau-Ponty are from Merleau-Ponty, *Le monde sensible et le monde de l'expression*, 96.

87. Georges Sadoul, *Dictionnaire des Films* [1965], updated by Émile Breton (Paris: Seuil, 1976); trans., ed., update, by Peter Morris, *Dictionary of*

Films (Berkeley, Los Angeles: University of California Press, 1972), 430 [trans. modified, *T.N.*].

88. See Merleau-Ponty, *Sense and Non-Sense*, 56.

89. Quoted in Sadoul, *Dictionary of Films*, 430.

90. Merleau-Ponty, *Le monde sensible et le monde de l'expression*, 119.

91. Ibid., 113.

92. On this subject, Merleau-Ponty writes in his course notes: "perceptual *logos* as such—(the body)." Ibid., 120.

93. Merleau-Ponty, "Themes from the Lectures at the Collège de France, 1952–1960," 74.

94. Merleau-Ponty, *Eye and Mind*, 145. I shall refer to the bond between this Merleau-Pontian phrase and the sequence from *Zéro de conduite* as it was exposed in Anna Caterina Dalmasso's article titled "Le médium visible. Interface opaque et immersivité non mimétique," *Chiasmi* 16 (2014): 109. Farther on, the same commentator has bound the Merleau-Pontian similitude of the metaphors by which Jean Epstein describes the effect of slow motion, in a passage of *The Intelligence of a Machine* that Merleau-Ponty quotes in *Le monde sensible et le monde de l'expression*, 116–17. See Anna Caterina Dalmasso, "Le médium visible. Interface opaque et immersivité non mimétique," 116, n. 89.

95. For an inquiry about some "crossings" between Merleau-Ponty's thought and the video-artistic activity of Bill Viola, see Isabel Matos Dias, "Croisement de regards. La phénoménologie de M. Merleau-Ponty et l'art vidéo de Bill Viola," *Daímon. Revista de Filosofía* 44 (Mayo–Agosto 2008): 85–92.

96. Merleau-Ponty, *Le monde sensible et le monde de l'expression*, 102. In the Introduction to *Signs*, he will write: "[T]he world and Being hold only in movement; it is only in thus was that all things can be together." Maurice Merleau-Ponty, *Signes* (Paris: Gallimard, 1960); trans. Richard C. McCleary, *Signs* (Evanston: Northwestern University Press, 1964), 22.

97. Maurice Merleau-Ponty, *Causeries 1948*, established and noted by Stéphanie Ménasé (Paris: Seuil, 2002); trans. Oliver Davis, "Art and the World of Perception," in Maurice Merleau-Ponty, *The World of Perception* (London-New York: Routledge, 2004), 97–98.

98. Ibid., 98.

99. To my knowledge, François Albera was the only one to report that "the programs of the 'Institut de filmologie' affiliated to the 'Université de Paris,' which were published on the fifth issue of the *Revue internationale de filmologie* (2nd year, 1949–1950) [. . .] mention Merleau-Ponty, professor at the 'Université de Lyon,' apropos of a lecture or a series of talks titled 'La signification au cinéma' [The Meaning in Cinema]" (Albera, "Maurice Merleau-Ponty et le cinéma," 124–25.) Albera himself gave me a preview of the notes taken by Marcel Martin, which will be published shortly in *1895 Revue d'histoire du cinema*. I thank him for that.

100. Differently from what happened in "The Cinema and The New Psychology" (see Merleau-Ponty, *Sense and Non-Sense*, 55–56 and 58), the name of André Malraux and his conception of cinema are never quoted in this course's theme and notes. Still, I find it appropriate to point out the convergence between the characterization of the cinema as art proposed in his course and what Malraux wrote in this issue in his *Esquisse d'une psychologie du cinéma*, published in 1940 on *Verve* and recalled by Merleau-Ponty precisely in his talk at the IDHEC (indeed, also in the 1948 *Causeries* there are echoes of this article by Malraux). On this issue, Malraux wrote in his article: "So long as the cinema served merely for the portrayal of figures in motion it was no more (and no less) an art than plain photography. Within a defined space, generally a real or imagined theatre stage, actors performed a play or a comic scene, which the camera merely recorded. The birth of the cinema as a means of expression (not of reproduction) dates from the abolition of that *defined space*." André Malraux, "Esquisse d'une psychologie du cinéma," *Verve* 8 (1940), trans. Susanne K. Langer, "Sketch for a Psychology of the Moving Pictures," in *Reflections on Art: A Source Book of Writing by Artists, Critics, and Philosophers*, ed. Susanne K. Langer (Baltimore: John Hopkins University Press, 1958), 320. And, a little farther, "The means of reproduction in the cinema is the moving photograph, but its means of expression is a sequence of *planes*." Ibid.

101. Merleau--Ponty, *In Praise of Philosophy and Other Essays*, 78 [translation modified (T.N.)].

102. Ibid., 79; my emphasis.

103. Merleau-Ponty, *Eye and Mind*, 129; my emphasis.

104. André Bazin, "Ontologie de l'image photographique" [1945]; trans. Hugh Gray, "The Ontology of the Photographic Image," *Film Quarterly* 13, no. 4 (Summer 1960): 9.

105. Merleau-Ponty, *Eye and Mind*, 129.

106. This is what Renaud Barbaras seems to miss when formulating the following judgment: "Just like Husserl, instead of questioning the subject *starting from* the perceptual relation, Merleau-Ponty tries to *build* the relation starting from a subject whose (empiric-transcendental) bipolarity is not profoundly enquired. The only overcoming with relation to Husserl consists in starting from an embodied subject, rather than from a transcendental subject." Renaud Barbaras, *Vie et intentionnalité. Recherches phénomenologiques* (Paris: Vrin, 2003), 156.

107. Merleau-Ponty, *The Visible and the Invisible*, 130.

108. Ibid., 146; my emphasis.

109. Ibid., 152.

110. "If one wants metaphors, it would be better to say that the body sensed and the body sentient are as the obverse and the reverse, or again, as two segments of one sole circular course which goes above from left to right

and below from right to left, but which is but one sole movement in its two phases." Ibid., 138.

111. Merleau-Ponty, *Eye and Mind*, 146.

112. Ibid., 126.

113. Ibid.

114. See Merleau-Ponty, *The Visible and the Invisible*, 141.

115. Jean-Luc Godard, *JLG/JLG. Phrases* (Paris: P. O. L., 1996), 69–71. On this subject, see Stefan Kristensen, "L'œil et l'esprit de Jean-Luc Godard," *Chiasmi International*, nouvelle série 12 (2010): 132 and following.

116. See Francesco Casetti, *L'occhio del Novecento. Cinema, esperienza, modernità* (Milano: Bompiani, 2005); trans. Erin Larkin and Jennifer Pranolo, *Eye of the Century: Film, Experience, Modernity* (New York: Columbia University Press, 2008), in particular 162, where on this issue Casetti refers precisely to the reflection of the later Merleau-Ponty. Some of the considerations I propose in the pages that follow are inspired by this book.

117. Merleau-Ponty, *Eye and Mind*, 139.

118. Ibid., 147.

119. Jean Baudrillard will in his turn characterize *simulacra* as *figures of precession*: "[I]t is the map that precedes the territory—*precession of simulacra*—it is the map that engenders the territory." Jean Baudrillard, "La précession des simulacres," in *Simulacres et simulations* (Paris: Galilee, 1981); trans. Paul Foss, Paul Patton, and Philip Beitchman, *Simulations* (New York: Semiotext(e), 1983), 2.

120. As for the occurrences of the word *precession* in Merleau-Ponty's unpublished notes, I shall mark the volume number of the Bibliothèque Nationale de France (BnF), the abbreviation of the unpublished writing, and indicate the BnF numbering for each note's sheet, followed, if any, by Merleau-Ponty's own numbering. Concerning this convention, see Emmanuel de Saint Aubert, *Du lien des être aux éléments de l'être: Merleau-Ponty au tournant des années 1945–1951* (Paris: Vrin, 2004), "Note technique et bibliographique," 9–10.

121. Rudolf Arnheim, *Art and Visual Perception* (Berkeley: University of California Press, 1954). Concerning this occurrence of the word *precession* in Merleau-Ponty's unpublished notes, see BnF, vol. XXI, NL-Arnh [53] (50).

122. These words are respectively translated as "infringement" and "encroachment" in Merleau-Ponty, *The Visible and the Invisible*, 134.

123. See BnF, vol. V, OE-ms [36]v(53) and [94](42).

124. BnF, vol. VII, NLVIàf3 [186].

125. BnF, vol. VII, NLVIàf3 [181].

126. Ibid.

127. It is not by chance that the Merleau-Pontian definition of vision that is examined here could be considered as the theoretical core of the convergence between the later Merleau-Ponty and Bazin. Pietro Montani could thus write:

"The truth is that Bazin, just like Merleau-Ponty, is a phenomenologist who had seen the ontological stake of imagination: that is, the emergence of the image from an 'ebb' and 'flow,' its constitution as a back and forth of vision from the things to the form and vice-versa, or of the data to sense and vice-versa." Pietro Montani, *L'immaginazione narrativa. Il racconto del cinema oltre i confini dello spazio letterario* (Milano: Guerini e Associati, 1999), 74.

128. Merleau-Ponty, *Eye and Mind*, 147.

129. Merleau-Ponty, *The Visible and the Invisible*, 243.

130. Ibid., 24.

131. See Georges Didi-Huberman, *Devant le temps. Histoire de l'art et anachronisme des images* (Paris: Minuit, 2000), 239–40.

132. Merleau-Ponty, *Notes de cours au Collège de France 1958–1959 et 1960–1961*, 115.

133. Merleau-Ponty, *Eye and Mind*, 130.

134. See Merleau-Ponty, *The Visible and the Invisible*, 149–51.

135. See Mauro Carbone, *Una deformazione senza precedenti. Marcel Proust e le idee sensibili* (Macerata: Quodlibet, 2004); trans. Niall Kane, *An Unprecedented Deformation. Marcel Proust and the Sensible Ideas* (Albany: State University of New York Press, 2010).

136. "Here, on the contrary, there is no vision without the screen: the ideas we are speaking of would not be better known to us if we had no body and no sensibility; it is then that they would be inaccessible to us." Merleau-Ponty, *The Visible and the Invisible*, 150.

137. We might say that that "smile [. . .] keeps producing and reproducing [. . .] on the surface of a canvas" like an image *and at once* like an essence. More precisely, following the expression that Merleau-Ponty uses a few lines below, like a "carnal essence."

138. Merleau-Ponty, *Eye and Mind*, 130.

139. Deleuze states something close to this idea in the last answer of the interview given to the *Cahiers du Cinéma* 380 (Feb. 1986), when he published *L'image-temps*: "That's funny, because it seems obvious to me that the [cinematic] image is not in the present. What the image 'represents' is in the present, but not the image itself. The image itself is an ensemble of time relations." Then he goes on echoing Proust: "On each occasion, it's 'a little time in the pure state,' and not in the present." Gilles Deleuze, Gregory Flaxman (ed.), "The Brain Is the Screen: An Interview with Gilles Deleuze," in *The Brain is the Screen: Deleuze and the Philosophy of Cinema* (Minneapolis: University of Minnesota Press, 2000), 371.

140. One could link the terms of this question also to the struggle of the painter to free his canvas from the "clichés" occupying it even *before* he begins painting. D. H. Lawrence refers to such a struggle, apropos of Cézanne, in a text ("Introduction to These Paintings" [1929]) recalled by Deleuze in his

book on Bacon in order to point out that the work of the painter does not consist in reproducing an exterior object, on a *white surface*. See G. Deleuze, *Francis Bacon. Logique de la sensation* (Paris: La différence, 1981); trans. Daniel W. Smith, *Francis Bacon: The Logic of Sensation* (Minneapolis: University of Minnesota Press, 2003), 61–62.

141. Merleau-Ponty, *In Praise of Philosophy and Other Essays*, 116. It is well known that, as for Deleuze, it is starting with the Italian Neorealism that "[w]e run in fact into a principle of indeterminability, of indiscernibility: we no longer know what is imaginary or real, physical or mental, in the situation, not because they are confused, but because we do not have to know and there is no longer even a place from which to ask. It is as if the real and the imaginary were running after each other, as if each was being reflected in the other, around a point of indiscernibility" (Deleuze, *Cinema 2*, 7). Forty pages farther, concerning this very relationship between the real and the imaginary, he adds: "*without it being possible to say which is first*" (Ibid., 46; my emphasis). For a comparative cinematographic analysis of Merleau-Ponty's and Deleuze's reflections on images, see O. Fahle, "La visibilité du monde. Deleuze, Merleau-Ponty et le cinéma," in A. Beaulieu (ed.), *Gilles Deleuze. Héritage philosophique* (Paris: P.U.F., 2005, 123–43).

142. Merleau-Ponty, *Eye and Mind*, 130.

143. The reference to this mutual precession is fundamental in order to understand in which sense Merleau-Ponty used the expressions *according to* (*selon*) and *with* (*avec*) as synonyms, even if, strictly speaking, they are not. The expression *according to*, etymologically meaning "following, in conformity with," it implies the reference to somebody else's preliminary initiative. In other words, it suggests once more a distinction of a preliminary and a secondary term, whilst the preposition *with* aims precisely at avoiding such a distinction, as well as the distinction of activity and passivity.

144. Deleuze, *Cinema 1*, xiv.

145. Cf. *supra*, 115–16, n. 51.

146. For Sartre, the cinema "renews the symbols." Sartre, "Apologie pour le cinema," 394; according to Merleau-Ponty, the cinema "has discovered [. . .] a new way of symbolizing thoughts." Merleau-Ponty, *In Praise of Philosophy*, 78.

147. Deleuze, *Cinema 1*, 182: "It might be said that the fundamental duality which characterised the action-image tends to go beyond itself towards a higher instance, as a 'thirdness' capable of converting the images and their elements. Take an example borrowed from Kant: the despotic State is directly presented in certain actions, such as a slave-based and mechanical organisation of labour; but the 'windmill' would be the indirect figuration in which that State is reflected. Eisenstein's method in *Strike* is exactly the same: the tsarist State is presented directly in the shooting of the demonstrators, but the abattoir is the indirect image, which both reflects that State and represents this action."

148. As far as Deleuze is concerned, see Ibid., xiv. See also Gilles Deleuze, "Qu'est-ce-que l'acte de création?" (1987), trans. Ames Hodges and Mike Taormina; "What Is the Creative Act?," in *Two Regimes of Madness: Texts and Interviews 1975–1995*, 312–24.

149. Merleau-Ponty, *Notes des cours au Collège de France 1958–1959 et 1960–1961*, 391.

150. Ibid.

151. Ibid.

152. Ibid., 163.

153. Ibid., 275.

154. The Kantian expression *conceptless* [*ohne Begriff*] appears at least thrice in the writings of the later Merleau-Ponty: see *Eye and Mind*, 133, 142; *The Visible and the Invisible*, 152 (here translated as "without concept").

155. Merleau-Ponty, *The Visible and the Invisible*, 102; translation modified.

156. On this subject, see my book *An Unprecedented Deformation*.

157. Merleau-Ponty, *The Visible and the Invisible*, 152; my emphasis.

158. Merleau-Ponty, *Notes des cours au Collège de France 1958–1959 et 1960–1961*, 194.

159. Merleau-Ponty, *The Visible and the Invisible*, 150.

160. Ibid., 149.

161. Ibid., 150.

162. "André Bazin ontology of cinema." Merleau-Ponty, *Notes des cours au Collège de France 1958–1959 et 1960–1961*, 391.

163. In what sense could we say that the writings of certain film critics are animated by a conceptless thought of the kind I have tried to characterize so far? In the sense that Deleuze imputes to Godard: "Godard likes to recall that, when the future directors of the new wave were writing, they were not writing about cinema, they were not making a theory out of it, it was already their way of making films." Deleuze, *Cinema 2*, 280.

164. Ibid., 1.

165. Gilles Deleuze, "*Sur L'image-temps*" (1985), in Deleuze, *Pourparlers: 1972–1990* (Paris: Minuit, 1990); trans. Martin Joughin, "On the Time-Image," in *Negotiations: 1972–1990* (New York: Columbia University Press, 1995), 57.

166. Deleuze, *Cinema 1*, xiv.

167. Deleuze, *Cinema 2*, 280.

168. Afterward, Deleuze will rather claim: "The only people capable of thinking effectively about cinema are the filmmakers and film critics or those who love cinema." "What Is the Creative Act?" in *Two Regimes of Madness*, 313.

169. "Philosophical theory [. . .] is no more abstract than its object." Deleuze, *Cinema 2*, 280.

170. On this subject, allow me to direct the reader to my contribution titled "Mais quelle 'création de concepts'?" in *La Géophilosophie de Gilles Deleuze*

entre esthétiques et politiques, ed. Mauro Carbone, Paride Broggi, Laura Turarbek (Paris: Mimesis France, 2012), 17–25.

171. See Deleuze, "Renverser le platonisme," *Revue de Métaphysique et de Morale* 4 (1967); republished under the title "Platon et le simulacre" in *Logique du sens* (Paris: Minuit, 1969), 292–307; trans. Mark Lester and Charles Stivale, "Plato and the Simulacrum," in *The Logic of Sense*, ed. Constantin V. Boundas (New York: Columbia University Press, 1990), 253–65.

172. See Deleuze, *Cinema 1*, ch. 12, in particular 202.

173. Slavoj Žižek, *Organs Without Bodies. Deleuze and Consequences* (New York: Routledge, 2004), 157.

174. Deleuze, *Cinema 2*, 280.

Chapter 3. The Torn Curtain

1. Merleau-Ponty, *Notes de cours au Collège de France 1958–1959 et 1960–1961*, 305. For reasons of consistency, I will translate the "Philosophy and Non-Philosophy since Hegel" course notes myself, even if an English translation is available (see M. Merleau-Ponty, "Philosophy and Non-Philosophy since Hegel," trans. and ed. Hugh J. Silverman, in *Philosophy and Non-Philosophy since Merleau-Ponty* [New York and London: Routledge, 1988], 9–83, here 40). T.N.

2. In the preparatory notes to the 1953 course we examined above, Merleau-Ponty points out that these two phenomena belong to "the same order." Merleau-Ponty, *Le monde sensible et le monde de l'expression*, 96. See also 95: "idea that movement = related with apprehension of figure on ground").

3. See *supra*, 122, n. 136.

4. This is why, concerning this subject, Merleau-Ponty writes, in *The Visible and the Invisible*, that the sensible ideas "are in transparency behind the sensible, or in its heart." Merleau-Ponty, *The Visible and the Invisible*, 150.

5. I am borrowing the term *acclimatization* from Mikel Dufrenne, *Phénoménologie de l'experience esthétique* (Paris: P. U. F., 1953); trans. Edward S. Casey, *Phenomenology of the Aesthetic Experience* (Evanston: Northwestern University Press, 1973), xiviii, note 2: "It will be seen that we are not striving to follow Husserl to the letter. We understand phenomenology in the sense in which Sartre and Merleau-Ponty have acclimated this term in France: a description which aims at an essence, itself defined as a meaning immanent in the phenomenon and given with it."

6. Jean-François Lyotard, *Discours, figure* (Paris: Klincksieck, 1971); trans. Anthony Hudek and Mary Lydon, *Discourse, Figure* (Minneapolis: University of Minnesota Press, 2011).

7. Apropos of the chiasm between the visible and the visual starting from Merleau-Ponty, see Vivian Sobchack's work, in particular her "The Visual

and the Visible: Toward a Phenomenology of the Film Experience," *Stanford Humanities Review* 2, no. 2–3 (1992): 109–28.

8. Lyotard, *Discourse, Figure*, 286.

9. Ibid., 328.

10. Ibid.

11. Merleau-Ponty, *The Visible and the Invisible*, 154.

12. Lyotard, *Discourse, Figure*, 286 (trans. modified, T.N.).

13. Besides, it is important to recall, as does Pierre Rodrigo, that "during the last ten years of his life, Merleau-Ponty has been questioning with an unbelievable constancy about the signification of the Freudian concept of libido." Pierre Rodrigo, "À la frontière du désir: la dimension de la libido chez Merleau-Ponty," in Rodrigo, *L'intentionnalité créatrice. Problèmes de phénoménologie et d'esthétique*, 51.

14. See Jean-François Lyotard, *Dérive à partir de Marx et de Freud* (Paris: Union Général d'Editions, 1973), and Lyotard, *Des dispositifs pulsionnels* (Paris: Union Général d'Editions, 1973).These two volumes have not been translated as such in English, but a miscellanea of some essays from the two books has been published in Jean-François Lyotard, *Driftworks*, ed. Roger McKeon (New York: Semiotext(e), 1984).

15. Jean-François Lyotard, "Notes sur la fonction critique de l'œuvre" (1970); trans. Susan Hanson, "Notes on the Critical Function of the Work of Art," in Lyotard, *Driftworks*, 71.

16. Jean-Michel Durafour, *Jean-François Lyotard: questions au cinéma* (Paris: P. U. F., 2009), 23.

17. Jean-François Lyotard, "L'acinéma," *Revue d'Esthétique* XXVI, no. 2–4 numéro spécial, *Cinéma: théorie, lectures*: 357–69; trans. Paisley N. Livingstone and the author, "Acinema," in *Wide Angle* 23 (1978): 52–91.

18. Ibid., 53.

19. Ibid., 57.

20. Ibid.

21. Jacques Lacan, "Le stade du miroir comme formateur de la fonction du Je telle qu'elle nous est révélée dans l'expérience psychanalytique" (1949), in Lacan, *Écrits* (Paris: Seuil, 1966), 93–100; trans. Bruce Fink, in collaboration with Heloise Fink and Russell Grigg, "The Mirror Stage as Formative of the *I* Function as Revealed in Psychoanalytic Experience," in Lacan, *Écrits. The First Complete Edition in English* (London/New York: Norton, 2002), 76–83.

22. Ibid., 77: "It suffices to understand the mirror stage in this context as an identification, in the full sense analysis gives to the term: namely, the transformation that takes place in the subject when he assumes [assume] an image."

23. See Jacques Lacan, "Du regard comme objet petit *a*," in Lacan, *Le séminaire de Jacques Lacan. Livre XI. Les quatre concepts fondamentaux de la psychanalyse*, ed. Jacques-Alain Miller (1964) (Paris: Seuil, 1973); trans. Alan Sheridan, "Of the Gaze as *Objet Petit a*," in Lacan, *The Seminar of Jacques Lacan.*

The Four Fundamental Concepts of Psychoanalysis (London/New York: Norton, 2002), 67–122.

24. Slavoj Žižek, *Organs Without Bodies. On Deleuze and Consequences* (New York/London: Routledge, 2004), 155.

25. Lacan, *Écrits*, 76.

26. As Jean-Louis Déotte points out by generally referring to "the members of *Socialisme ou Barbarie* (Castoriadis, Lefort, Lyotard, Morin, etc.)," "the risk taken by these theoreticians coming from Freudianism is to turn the socio-political into a body shaped after the model of the individual body, and hence to transfer the psychoanalytic assumption on the political, which is not issueless." Jean-Louis Déotte, "L'acinéma de J.-F. Lyotard," *Revue Apparel* (online), no. 6 (2010), updated 06/01/2011, http://appareil.revues.org/973, 1.

27. Lyotard, "Acinema," 57.

28. Jean-François Lyotard, "Freud selon Cézanne" (1971), in *Des dispositifs pulsionnels* (Paris: Union Général d'Editions, 1973); trans. Ashley Woodward and John Roffe, "Freud According to Cézanne," in *Parrhesia* 23 (2015): 26–42.

29. Ibid., 33.

30. Ibid.

31. Ibid.

32. Ibid., 29.

33. Ibid.

34. See S. Freud, *Eine kindheitserinnerung des Leonardo da Vinci* (Leipzig and Vienna: Deuticke, 1910); trans. Abraham Arden Brill, *Leonardo da Vinci and a Memory of His Childhood* (New York: Barnes and Noble, 2003).

35. Lyotard, "Freud According to Cézanne," 28.

36. Jean-François Lyotard, "Peinture et désir," delivered at the Sorbonne on December 9, 1972; trans. Vlad Ionescu, Erica Harris, Peter W. Milne, "Painting and Desire," in Lyotard, *Miscellaneous Texts I: Aesthetics and Theory of Art*, ed. Herman Parret (Leuven: Leuven University Press, 2011), 53.

37. On this subject, see Gérard Wajcman, *Fenêtre: croniques du regard et de l'intime* (Lagrasse: Verdier, 2004), and Anne Friedberg, *The Virtual Window: From Alberti to Microsoft* (Cambridge: MIT Press, 2006).

38. Lyotard precisely talks about a "veil of representations," see Lyotard, "Freud According to Cézanne," 28.

39. Ibid., 38.

40. Ibid., 29 (trans. modified, T.N.); the first emphasis is mine.

41. Jean-François Lyotard, "Notes on the Critical Function of the Work of Art," in Lyotard, *Driftworks*, 73.

42. Ibid.

43. Ibid., 71.

44. See Ibid., 74.

45. Ibid., 72.

46. Ibid., 82.

47. The reference to the Freudian characterization of the *jouissance* appears also in the "Acinema" essay. See Lyotard, "Acinema," 54–55.

48. Ibid., 57.

49. Ibid., 54.

50. Ibid.

51. Ibid., 57.

52. Twenty-two years later, in November 1995, when concluding a talk delivered in Munich and titled "Idée d'un film souverain [The Idea of a Sovereign Film]," Lyotard will posit the following self-comprehension of his thesis on the acinema: "I think that a movie director, if he is not a seller of images, brings forward the idea of a sovereign film in which, at certain times, the realistic scenario makes room for the presence of the ontological real. Such an idea needs to remain an Idea in Kant's sense, that is, a conception to which no object, in this case no film, can ever correspond in experience. There is no sovereign film, for sovereignty is incompatible with an objective totality," Jean-François Lyotard, *Misère de la philosophie* (Paris: Galilée, 2000), 211.

53. Lyotard, "Acinema," 59.

54. Jean-François Lyotard, "Notes on the Critical Function of the Work of Art," in Lyotard, *Driftworks*, 75.

55. Durafour, *Jean-François Lyotard: questions au cinéma*, 26: "What differentiates the acinema and the cinema fundamentally concerns movement."

56. Ibid., 78 and 79.

57. See *supra*, 46, Lyotard's passage to which note 40 makes reference.

58. See Merleau-Ponty, *Eye and Mind*, 126.

59. Lyotard, "Acinema," 56. The film Lyotard refers to is John Avildsen's *Joe* (USA, 1970).

60. See Durafour, *Jean-François Lyotard: questions au cinéma*, 30.

61. Lyotard, "Acinema," 57; trans. modified, *T.N*.

62. Merleau-Ponty mentions Lacan's mirror stage with reference to Schilder's "libidinal structure of the body schema." As he writes, "[t]he total explicitation of the body schema provides not only the relation of the subject to itself, but also its relation to others: in my body schema are already included some presentations of myself that can only be obtained from the other's point of view (my face seen in front): event of one's self vision is event of the other (mirror stage)" (see Merleau-Ponty, *Le monde sensible et le monde de l'expression*, 159, and Lacan, "The Mirror Stage as Formative of the *I* Function as Revealed in Psychoanalytic Experience").

63. Merleau-Ponty, *Eye and Mind*, 145.

64. Lyotard, *Discourse, Figure*, 19.

65. On this subject, see also Déotte, "L'acinéma de J.-F. Lyotard," 4.

66. Lyotard, "Freud According to Cézanne," 29.

67. Ibid., 39.
68. Ibid., 40.
69. Jean-François Lyotard, *La condition postmoderne: rapport sur le savoir* (Paris: Minuit, 1979); trans. Geoff Bennington and Brian Massumi, *The Postmodern Condition: A Report on Knowledge* (Minneapolis: University of Minnesota Press, 1984 [Theory and History of Literature, vol. 10, Manchester: Manchester University Press, 1989]).
70. Ibid., 3.
71. Ibid., xxiii.
72. Lyotard, "Freud According to Cézanne," 29.
73. Jean-François Lyotard, *Les immatériaux. Album* (Paris: Éditions du Centre Georges Pompidou, 1985), 18.
74. Ibid., 26–27.
75. "Lyotard's aim is hence not to situate the acinema in a questionable *extra*, but rather to think of it as to what is *infiltrated in the figurative cinema*." Durafour, *Jean François Lyotard: questions au cinéma*, 65.
76. Cf. Ibid., 26. The expression is taken from the title of Charles Musser's book *The Emergence of Cinema* (New York: Charles Scribner's Sons, 1990).
77. However, such a historical mutation seems to be seen by Jean Renoir when he points out the reversal that the importance of the lighting of a show had for his father, the painter, and for himself, the filmmaker. Jean Renoir, *Pierre Auguste Renoir, mon père* (Paris: Hachette, 1962), 203. On the same subject, see also Giuliana Bruno, *Surface: Matters of Aesthetics, Materiality, and Media* (Chicago: University of Chicago Press, 2014), 121.
78. See Durafour, *Jean-François Lyotard: questions au cinéma*, 61–63, and Vivian Sobchack, "The Scene of the Screen: Envisioning Photographic, Cinematic, and Electronic 'Presence'" (1994), in *Carnal Thoughts: Embodiment and Moving Image Culture* (Berkeley/Los Angeles/London: University of California Press, 2004), 142, note 14.
79. On this synaesthetic configuration, see my *An Unprecedented Deformation*, 90, note 43.
80. Sobchack, *Carnal Thoughts*, 136.
81. Fredric Jameson, *Postmodernism, Or, The Cultural Logic of Late Capitalism* [1984] (Durham: Duke University Press, 1991). From now on, I choose to use the word *postmodernism* as Jameson does, just to name a recent Western historic and cultural phase that was inaugurated by a number of mutations making such a phase irreducible to the previous period. In any case, my concern is to avoid as much as possible the multiple and often deceiving ideological connotations that have been positively or negatively attributed to this notion. I have tried to overview the essential themes of the debate on modernism and postmodernism in the introduction and in the first chapter of my *Être morts ensemble*, French

trans. Marc Logoz (Geneva: MētisPresses, 2013). Besides, in the same volume, I explained that Jan Patočka also claims that mutations capable of marking an epochal change can be spotted more or less in the very period indicated by Lyotard and Jameson. With respect to this, Patočka talks about a "post-european age;" see Jan Patočka, "Europa und Nach-Europa. Die nacheuropäische Epoche und ihre geistigen Probleme," in Jan Patočka, *Ketzerische Essais zur Philosophie der Geschichte und ergänzende Schriften, Ausgewählte Schriften*, vol. II, eds. Klaus Nellen and Jiri Němec, preface by Paul Ricoeur (Stuttgart: Klett-Cotta, 1988), 207–87. See also the Fourth Chapter of Mauro Carbone, *Être morts ensemble*, French trans. Marta Nijhuis, 103–12).

82. Sobchack, *Carnal Thoughts*, 140.

83. Ibid.

84. Slavoj Žižek, *How to Read Lacan* (London: Granta, 2006), 67.

85. See Friedrich Nietzsche, "Wie die 'wahre Welt' endlich zur Fabel wurde. Geschichte eines Irrthums," in *Götzen-Dämmerung, oder, Wie man mit dem Hammer philosophirt* [1889] (Leipzig: Alfred Kröner Verlag, 1922); trans. Reginald John Hollingdale, "How the Real World Last Became a Myth: History of an Error," in *Twilight of the Idols, Or How to Philosophize With a Hammer; The Anti-Christ* (London: Penguin Classics, 1968), 40–41.

86. Slavoj Žižek, *How to Read Lacan*, 72.

87. Ibid.

88. The attacks of 9/11 against the United States, which I will evoke in the last chapter of the present book, have been diagnosed by Jean Baudrillard and by Jacques Derrida as an autoimmune crisis of the West. On this subject, I shall once more refer to my book *Être morts ensemble*. Besides, it should be recalled that certain theses of Jan Patočka's *Heretical Essays in the Philosophy of History* have been resumed by Paul Ricœur as "the suicide of Europe in the two great world wars." Paul Ricœur, "Préface," in Jan Patočka, *Essais hérétiques sur la philosophie de l'histoire*, French trans. Erika Abrams (Paris: Verdier, 1981); trans. Erazim Kohak, ed. James Dodd, Paul Ricœur, "Preface," in Jan Patočka, *Heretical Essays in the Philosophy of History* (Chicago: Open Court, 1996), viii.

Chapter 4. Delimiting to Exceed

1. Walter Benjamin, "Das Kunstwerk im Zeitalter seiner technischen Reproduzierbarkeit" [1936]; trans. Edmund Jephcott and Harry Zohn, ed. Michael W. Jennings, Brigid Doherty, and Thomas Y. Levin, "The Work of Art in the Age of its Technological Reproducibility," in *The Work of Art in the Age of Its Technological Reproducibility, and Other Writings on Media* (Cambridge: Harvard University Press, 2008), 53.

2. See Walter Benjamin, *Werke und Nachlaß. Kritische Gesamtausgabe*, hrsg. von Christoph Gödde und Henri Lonitz (Berlin: Suhrkamp, 2008), vol. XCI: *Das Kunstwerk im Zeitalter seiner technischen Reproduzierbarkeit*, hrsg. von Burkhardt Lindner unter Mitarbeit von Simon Broll und Jessica Nitsche, 2012, 317.

3. See Edward S. Casey, *The World at a Glance* (Bloomington and Indianapolis: Indiana University Press, 2007), in particular 482–83.

4. Ibid., 133.

5. Ibid.

6. Leon Battista Alberti, *Della Pittura* [1435–36], Libro primo, § 19, trans. Rocco Sinigalli, *On Painting: A New Translation and Critical Edition* (Cambridge: Cambridge University Press, 2011), 39; my emphasis.

7. Albrecht Dürer, "Underweysung der Messung mit dem Zirkel und Richtscheyt" [1525], trans. Walter S. Strauss, in *The Painter's Manual: A Manual of Measurement of Lines, Areas, and Solids by Means of Compass and Ruler Assembled by Albrecht Dürer for the Use of All Lovers of Art with Appropriate Illustrations Arranged to be Printed in the Year MDXXV* (New York: Abaris Books, 1977).

8. Hans Belting, *Florence and Baghdad: Renaissance Art and Arab Science* (Cambridge: Harvard University Press, 2011), 242.

9. Ibid., my emphasis. Besides, it is important to recall that McLuhan also points out that "[e]very culture and every age has its favorite model of perception and knowledge that it is inclined to prescribe for everybody and everything." Marshall McLuhan, *Understanding Media. The Extensions of Man* [1964], Critical Edition by Terrence Gordon (Corte Madera, CA: Gingko Press 2003), 7.

10. Erwin Panofsky, "Die Perspektive als 'symbolische Form,'" in *Vorträge der Bibliothek Warburg 1924/1925* (Leipzig/ Berlin, 1927); trans. Christopher S. Wood, *Perspective as Symbolic Form* (New York: Zone Books, 1991), 27 and 76, N. 5.

11. For this consideration about the window, see first of all Wajcman, *Fenêtre*. See also Louise Charbonnier, *Cadre et regard: généalogie d'un dispositif* (Paris: L'Harmattan, 2007), particularly the chapter titled "Cadre et fenêtre, un dispositif pour la vision," 73 ff.

12. Marc Richir, "La défenestration," dans *L'arc*, numéro spécial "Merleau-Ponty," no. 46 (1971): 31–42.

13. René Descartes, *Méditations métaphysiques* [1641–1647]; trans. Elisabeth S. Haldane and George Robert Thomson Ross, "Meditations on First Philosophy," in Descartes, *Discourse on Method and Meditations* (Mineola, NY: Dover, 2003; reprint of the 1911 Cambridge University Press first edition), 78.

14. Richard Rorty explains this in the following terms: "In the Cartesian model, the intellect *inspects* entities modeled on retinal images [. . .]. In Descartes's conception—the one which became the basis for 'modern'—it is *representations* which are in the 'mind.'" Richard Rorty, *Philosophy and the Mirror of Nature* (Princeton: Princeton University Press, 1949), 45.

15. Richir, "La défenestration," 32.

16. Benjamin, "The Work of Art."

17. See Michel Foucault, "Le jeu de Foucault" (1977), in *Dits et écrits 1954–1988*, vol. IV: 1976–1979, ed. Daniel Defert and François Ewald with Jacques Lagrange (Paris: Gallimard, 1994); trans. Colin Gordon, Leo Marshall, John Mepham, Kate Soper, "The Confession of the Flesh," in Foucault, *Power / Knowledge. Selected Interviews and Other Writings 1972–1977*, ed. Colin Gordon (New York: Pantheon Books), 194.

18. Michel Foucault, *L'usage des plaisirs* (Paris: Gallimard, 1984); vol. 1, trans. Robert Hurley, *The Use of Pleasure* (New York: Vintage Books, 1985), 35.

19. Gilles Deleuze, "Qu'est-ce que un dispositif?" (1989), in *Deux régimes de fous. Textes et entretiens 1975–1995*, ed. David Lapoujade (Paris: Minuit, 2003); trans. Ames Hodges and Mike Taormina, "What Is a Dispositif?" in *Two Regimes of Madness. Texts and Interviews 1975–1995* (New York: Semiotext(e), 2006), 339.

20. Benjamin, "The Work of Art," 23.

21. Ibid.

22. Ibid.

23. "The desire to see has turned into the will of seeing everything." Gérard Wajcman, *L'œil absolu* (Paris: Denoël, 2010), 13.

24. See Mauro Carbone, "Falling Man: The Time of Trauma, the Time of (Certain) Images," in *Research in Phenomenology* 47 (2017): 190–203.

25. Gilles Deleuze, *Sur Nietzsche et l'image de la pensée* (1968), in *L'île deserte. Textes et entretiens 1953–1974*, ed. David Lapoujade (Paris: Minuit, 2002); trans. Michael Taormina, "On Nietzsche and the Image of Thought," in *Desert Islands and Other Texts (1953–74)* (New York: Semiotext(e), 2004), 139. "The Image of Thought" (*L'image de la pensée*) is the title of the "Conclusion to Part One" of the first edition of *Marcel Proust et les signes* (Paris: P. U. F., 1964); trans. Richard Howard, *Proust and Signs* (London/New York: Continuum, 2008), 60 ff. It is also the title of a chapter of *Différence et répétition* (Paris: P. U. F., 1968); trans. Paul Patton, *Difference and Repetition* (London/New York: Continuum, 2004), 164 ff.

26. Charbonnier, *Cadre et regard*, 19.

27. See Alberti, *On Painting*, Book II, § 31.

28. Lev Manovich, *The Language of New Media* (Cambridge: The MIT Press, 2000), 80–81.

29. Ibid., 95.

30. Daniel Arasse, *Histoires de peinture* (Paris: France Culture/Denoël, 2004), 63–64; my emphasis.

31. Ibid., 64.

32. Charbonnier, *Cadre et regard*, 30.

33. "As we know, Benjamin speaks of the 'decline of the aura' in the modern age, but for him, *decline* does not mean disappearance. Rather, it means (as in

the Latin *declinare*) moving downward, inclining, deviating, or inflecting in a new way." Georges Didi-Huberman, *Devant le temps. Histoire de l'art et anachronisme des images* (Paris: Minuit, 2000), 234; trans. of this passage by Jean-Marie Todd from Georges Didi-Huberman, "The Supposition of the Aura: The Now, the Then, and Modernity," in *Walter Benjamin and History*, ed. Andrew Benjamin (London/New York: Continuum, 2005), 4. My idea according to which screens solicit a form of contemplation that is declined in a different way rather than the impossibility to contemplate seems corroborated by Edward Casey when he remarks that "my gaze is invested in the act of contemplation itself, not in its object." Casey, *The World at a Glance*, 133. Hence, its object can be an image, no matter whether fixed or in motion.

34. See Aeschylus, *Agamemnon*, v. 117. On the same topic see also Euripides, *Heracles*, v. 596.

35. "*Templum* is the same word as the Greek τέμενος, from τέμνω, to cut off, for *templum*, according to Servius (*ad Aen*. I.446), was any place which was circumscribed and separated by the augurs from the rest of the land by a certain solemn formula." William Smith, *A Dictionary of Greek and Roman Antiquities* [1875] (Cambridge: Cambridge University Press, 2013), *s. v. templum*). Concerning the various meanings of the term *templum*, see Varro, *De lingua Latina*, VII 2.

36. See Iamblichus, *De vita pythagorica*, 71–73.

37. Merleau-Ponty, *Eye and Mind*, 127.

38. Audrey Rieber, *Arts et mythes des origines. Vingt ans d'interprétation de l'art pariétal paléolithique depuis la découverte de la grotte Chauvet*, in *Les Cahiers du Musée National d'Art Moderne* no. 126, "Préhistoire et modernité," ed. Rémi Labrousse, Maria Stavrinaki (hiver 2013–14): 83.

39. Werner Herzog, *Cave of Forgotten Dreams* (Canada, USA, France, Germany, UK, 2010).

40. Marc Azéma, *La Préhistoire du cinéma* (Arles: Errance, 2011), 21.

41. Bernard Stiegler, *La technique et le temps 3. Le temps du cinéma et la question du mal-être* (Paris: Galilée, 2001), 24. The notion of "arche-cinema" or "*consciousness cinema*" is based once more on the assumption that its nature "is *already cinematographic*" (Ibid., 41): the Bergsonian echo of this latter expression recalls the analysis of such a consideration as it has been developed in the first part of the present book.

42. See Pliny the Elder, *Natural History*, Book XXXV, § 151. Still concerning the subject of the body as proto-screen, it can be recalled that Michel Lorblanchet evokes the use of *"hands serving as screens"* in order to direct the pigment in the realization of" certain rupestrian images "by means of the *crachis* technique." Michel Lorblanchet, *Art pariétal. Grottes ornées du Quércy* (Rodez: Éditions du Rouergue, 2010), 114; my emphasis. In order to illustrate the same technique, he also mentions "the use of a leather screen with a central hole," and notices that it "may allow a higher precision with respect to the screen-hand"

(116). It could hence be affirmed that such a screen functioned as a sort of *prosthesis* of the screen-hand. Apropos of this acceptation of the word *prosthesis*, see the last chapter of the present book.

43. See S. Lojkine, "De l'allégorie à la scène: la Vierge-tabernacle," in B. Pérez-Jean et P. Eichel-Lojkine (eds.), *L'Allégorie de l'Antiquité à la Renaissance*, Paris, Champion, 2004, 509–531.

44. See in particular Carbone, *An Unprecedented Deformation*.

45. On the possible historical origins of the Cave imagined by Plato, the following essay is particularly interesting in the light of the topics discussed so far: John Henry Wright, *The Origin of Plato's Cave*, in "Harvard Studies in Classical Philology," Vol. 17 (1906), 131–42. Wright moves on from the assumption according to which "[i]t is hardly possible that this picture originated in pure imagination, borrowing no suggestion whatever from without, though imagination must have had much to do in the development of it." (132). Wright then particularly takes into account a cave devoted to Pan and the Nymphs on the slopes of the Hymettus by the village of Vari (accurately explored in 1901 by American archeologists), which presents many of the characteristics of Plato's own Cave (see 140–41 for the description of the place). According to Aelianus and Olympiodorus (see 141–42), Plato would have visited the cave as a child, with his parents. Although what has been found in this cave does not date back farther than 600 BCE, what Wright reports, quoting the account written by the archeologist in charge of the 1901 exploration of the cave, remains astonishing: "The raised platform, which is in many respects one of the most interesting features of the cave, [. . .] 'would have been a suitable place for the stately dances, possibly past the altar of Pan as portrayed in several of the reliefs. The darkness of the grotto with its flickering lights would have made such a worship weird and impressive in the highest degree'" (141).

46. See Plato, *Republic* 515 a-b.

47. See Ibid., 515b.

48. "Plato [. . .] indicates the possibility of achieving by reflection a version of the sound shadow theatre, an apparatus that its previous creatures practiced by transmission." Claudine Ezykman, Guy Fihman, "L'œil de Lyotard, de 'L'acinéma' au postmoderne," in *À partir de Jean-François Lyotard*, ed. Claude Amey, Jean-Paul Olive (Paris: L'Harmattan, 2000), 128.

49. See Plato, *Republic*, 514b.

50. See Henry Liddell, Robert Scott, Henry Stuart Jones, A *Greek-English Lexicon* (Oxford: Clarendon Press, 1940), "παράφραγμα."

51. See Plato, *Republic*, 514b.

52. See Liddell, Scott, Jones, A *Greek-English Lexicon*, "παράφραγμα," "φράσσω."

53. See Lesley Brown, ed., *The New Shorter Oxford English Dictionary* (Oxford: Clarendon Press, 1973), "screen." I will recall this as well as other fundamental elements of the history of this term in § 5 of the present chapter.

54. Merleau-Ponty, *Phenomenology of Perception*, 333.

55. Sigmund Freud, "Die Verneinung," *Imago* 11, no. 3 (1925); also translated into English: "Negation," in *The Standard Edition of the Complete Psychological Works of Sigmund Freud*, vol. 19, trans. and ed. James Strachey (London: Hogarth Press, 1953–1974), 235.

56. Concerning this issue, a crucial reference is Pierre Hadot's book, *Le voile d'Isis. Essai sur l'histoire de l'idée de Nature* (Paris: Gallimard, 2004); trans. Michael Chase, *The Veil of Isis: An Essay on the History of the Idea of Nature* (Cambridge/London:The Belknap Press of Harvard University Press, 2006).

57. Immanuel Kant, *Kritik der Urteilskraft* [1790]; trans. Paul Guyer and Eric Matthews, ed. Paul Guyer, *Critique of the Power of Judgment* (Cambridge: Cambridge University Press, 2000), 194, footnote.

58. "At Sais the seated statue of Athena, whom they consider to be Isis also, bore the following inscription: 'I am all that has been and will be; and no mortal has ever lifted my mantle.'" Plutarch, *De Iside et Osiride*, chapter 9. 354c, ed., introd., trans., and comm. John Gwyn Griffiths (Cardiff: University of Wales Press, 1970), 131.

59. Ibid., 241 (ch. 77. 382c).

60. See Ibid., 131 (ch. 9. 354c).

61. Merleau-Ponty, *The Visible and the Invisible*, 150. See *supra*, 122, n. 136.

62. Ibid.; my emphasis. Indeed, the arche-screenic feature of our bodily and hence sensible experience seems to be traceable in Kant's *Critique of the Power of Judgment* when he writes that "beauty is valid only for human beings, i. e. animal but also rational beings, but not merely as the latter (e.g., spirits), rather as beings who are at the same time animal" (Kant, *Critique of the Power of Judgment*, §5, 95).

63. In her book, significantly titled *Le corps c'est l'écran. La philosophie du visuel chez Merleau-Ponty* (*The Body Is the Screen. Philosophy of the Visual in Merleau-Ponty*), Anna Caterina Dalmasso finds in Merleau-Ponty's *Nature* a definition of the body "as a species of circumscription of space: just as the Roman augur traced a holy and meaningful contour, so does the organism define a *templum* where events will have an organic signification." Maurice Merleau-Ponty, *Nature*, 146; cited by Anna Caterina Dalmasso, *Le corps c'est l'écran. La philosophie du visuel chez Merleau-Ponty* (Milan-Paris: Mimesis, 2018), 232.

64. I characterized this imagination as "Mnemosyne" in my book *An Unprecedented Deformation*, 66.

65. For an approach to literature based on the notion of screen (but I could even say "arche-screen"), see Stéphane Lojkine's research. In his "Introduction" to *L'écran de la représentation*, he points out that such an approach "supposes the passage from a linear and textual modelization [. . .] to a spatial and iconic modelization that would integrate the primacy of image on language, of the medium to the signifier." (S. Lojkine [ed]., *L'écran de la représentation. Théorie littéraire. Littérature et peinture du 16ème au 20ème siècle* [Paris: L'Harmattan, 2001], 37).

66. Leopardi employs the same verb *"mirare"* that was used by Alberti when he translated the verb *contueor* from the Latin version of his treatise *On Painting* into the vernacular. As we know, Arasse proposes to treat the meaning of this Latin verb as "to contemplate."

67. Giacomo Leopardi, "L'infinito," in Id., *Canti* (Napoli: Saverio Starita, 1830); trans. Jonathan Galassi, "Infinity," in Leopardi, *Canti* (New York: Farrar Straus Giroux, 2019), 106.

68. Vilém Flusser warns against the "dangerous anachronism" consisting in including the "prehistoric universe" in the "history of images." Indeed, in his opinion, one can properly speak of a "history of images" "only since linear texts appeared." See Vilém Flusser, *Ins Universum der technischen Bilder* (Göttingen: European photography, 1985); trans. Nancy Ann Roth, *Into the Universe of Technical Images* (Minneapolis/London: University of Minnesota Press, [1985] 2011), 12–13.

69. Merleau-Ponty, "Eye and Mind," 126.

70. Kant, *Critique of the Power of Judgment*, 156.

71. Friedrich Nietzsche, "Die Fröhliche Wissenschaft," in *Sämtliche Werke, Kritische Studienausgabe* (KSA), vol. 3, ed. Giorgio Colli and Mazzino Montinari (Berlin: Walter de Gruyter, 1980). For the English version see *The Gay Science: With a Prelude in German Rhymes and an Appendix of Songs*, trans. Josefine Nauckhoff, ed. Bernard Williams (Cambridge: Cambridge University Press, 2001), 8.

72. Merleau-Ponty, *Signes*, 20–21. On this sentence and its consequences, see my book *The Flesh of Images*, 3 ff.

73. See, for instance, once again Lev Manovich, "With VR, the Screen Disappears Altogether," in Manovich, *The Language of New Media*, 101.

74. See Belting, *Florence and Baghdad*, 244.

75. See Georges Teyssot, "Fenêtres et écrans: entre intimité et extimité," *Revue Appareil* (on line), Articles, Varia, last consulted on April 4, 2018, http://appareil.revues.org/1005, 1–2.

76. Giorgio Agamben, *Che cos'è un dispositivo?* (Roma: Nottetempo, 2006); trans. David Kishik and Stefan Pedatella, "What Is an Apparatus?" in *What Is an Apparatus and Other Essays* (Stanford: Stanford University Press, 2009), 11.

77. Wajcman, *Fenêtre*, 14.

78. "What Is a Dispositif?" in *Two Regimes of Madness. Texts and Interviews 1975–1995*, 341.

79. See for instance André Bazin, "Théâtre et cinéma" [1951], in *Qu'est ce que le cinéma?* (Paris: Cerf, 2010); trans. Hugh Gray, "Theater and cinema," in *What Is Cinema?* (Berkeley/Los Angeles/London: University of California Press, 1967), 107.

80. Hitchcock described to Truffaut how *Rear Window* is constructed in the following way: "You have an immobilized man looking out. That's

one part of the film. The second part shows what he sees and the third part shows how he reacts. This is actually the purest expression of a *cinematic idea*." After this, as Merleau-Ponty had done in turn, Hitchcock reminds us of the Kuleshov effect. François Truffaut, *Le cinéma salon Alfred Hitchcock* (Paris: éditions Ramsay, 1983); English edition first published by Simon and Shuster (New York: 1984), here: revised edition of *Hitchcock. The Definitive Study of Alfred Hitchcock by François Truffaut* (London: Faber and Faber, 2017), 214; my emphasis. The window optical apparatus, for its part, would only allow to show *one* of these three parts.

81. By saying "literally," Carbone makes reference to the modern Latin etymology of the word *defenestration*, which is composed of *de-* ("down from") and *fenestra* ("window") (*T.N.*).

82. The same opinion was expressed by Friedberg, *The Virtual Window*, 6.

83. See the *Dictionnaire historique de la langue française*, dir. Alain Rey (Paris: Le Robert, 1998), tome II, 302.

84. Giorgio Agamben, "Dal libro allo schermo," in *Il fuoco e il racconto* (Roma: Nottetempo, 2014); trans. Lorenzo Chiesa, "From the Book to the Screen" in *The Fire and the Tale* (Stanford: Stanford University Press: 2017), 106. For a synthesis of these and other decisive elements in the history of the analyzed term, see Francesco Casetti, *The Lumière Galaxy: Seven Key Words for the Cinema to Come* (New York: Columbia University Press, 2015), 157 ff.

85. See Erkki Huhtamo, "Elements of Screenology: Toward an Archaeology of the Screen," in *Iconics: International Studies of Modern Image* (Tokyo: The Japan Society of Image Arts and Sciences) VII: 35.

86. "This ambiguity cannot be found in German (for example). Indeed, *Abschirmung*, which has a similar sense to *Wand*, i.e. 'wall,' cannot be confused with *Schirm*, which is related to 'screen' and '*écran*,' and designates objects that have a protective function. Still, the composed terms *Leinwand* (literally, 'wall, linen screen') or *Bildschirm* (*Bild* is the image) mark a comparable transition." *Dictionnaire historique de la langue française*, tome II, 303.

87. See Huhtamo, "Elements of Screenology," 39.

88. Merleau-Ponty, *Eye and Mind*, 296.

89. Hadot, *The Veil of Isis*, 271.

90. Ibid., 238.

91. "It suffices to recall the well-known scene from *Psycho* where Norman Bates nervously observes the car containing Marion's body submerging in the swamp behind his mother's house: when the car stops sinking for a moment, the anxiety that automatically arises in the viewer—a token of his/her solidarity with Norman—suddenly reminds him that his/her desire is identical to Norman's." Slavoj Žižek, "In His Bold Gaze My Ruin Is Writ Large," in Slavoj Žižek, ed., *Everything You Always Wanted to Know about Lacan (but Were Afraid to Ask Hitchcock)* (London / New York: Verso, 1992), 223.

92. See *supra*, 123, n. 143. When one looks deeper, the "contemplative attitude" (Hadot, *The Veil of Isis*, 317) with respect to "the veil of Isis" is an emblematic variation of such desire.

93. It is well known that Benjamin tends to see a structural opposition between theater and cinema, since the latter is exclusively conceived for the technical reproduction. See Benjamin, "The Work of Art," § 11.

94. See Belting, *Florence and Baghdad*, 246.

95. This distinction is at the basis of "the deep difference between the cinema and the television" according to Gilbert Simondon. See Gilbert Simondon, "Psychologie du cinéma" (inédit, daté 1960), in *Sur la technique (1953–1983)* (Paris: P. U. F., 2014), 359, from which the previous quotation is also drawn.

96. The phenomenon of the "Gulliverisation of media" is qualified as such, and reconstituted in some of the aspects of its archeology, by Erkki Huhtamo in the section titled "Enlarging and Shrinking: the Gulliverisation of Media" in his essay, "Messages on the Wall: An Archaeology of Public Media Displays," in *Urban Screens Reader,* ed. Scott McQuire, Meredith Martin, and Sabine Niederer (Amsterdam: Institute of Network Cultures, 2009), 15 ff., esp. 19–21.

97. See Plato, *Republic*, 603a.

98. Roland Barthes, "En sortant du cinéma," in "Communications" 23 (1975); trans. Richard Howard, "Leaving the Movie Theater," in *The Art of the Personal Essay*, ed. Phillip Lopate (New York: Anchor Books, 1995), 419.

99. See Luc Vancheri, "L'image-écran," in *Écrans* 1, Lyon 2–Lyon 3, L'Harmattan, 2013, 18 ff., and Pietro Montani, *Bioestetica. Senso comune, tecnica e arte nell'età della globalizzazione* (Roma: Carocci, 2007); French trans. Jean-Christophe Cavallin, *Bioesthétique. Sens commun, technique et art à l'âge de la globalisation* (Paris: Vrin, 2013), 155.

Chapter 5. Come Live with Me

1. These elements of interpretation of Porter's film converge with those Francesco Casetti posited in *Eye of the Century. Film, Experience, Modernity*, 144 ff. It is interesting to observe that such a convergence is reached starting from two totally different points of view: for Casetti, the point of view is Uncle Josh's, apropos of which he talks about "an ambiguous [. . .] [attraction] that can incite fear. The spectacle he sees on the screen causes Josh to flee (the train episode) as well as to penetrate deeper (the other two episodes in which Josh attempts to participate)" (146). In my case, the point of view is rather the screen's, which I characterize by speaking in terms of *seduction, promise, threat*.

2. The notion of seduction to which I am referring here is evoked by Sherry Turkle in order to analyze, more specifically, our relationships with com-

puters. See Sherry Turkle, *Life on the Screen: Identity in the Age of the Internet* (New York: Simon and Schuster, 1995), 30 ff.

3. It has to be noticed that, consistently with the interpretation of *Rear Window* I posited earlier, Clélia Zernik recalls that "[e]ventually, pushed by Thorwald, Jeffries ends up falling out of the window, hence hanging, properly speaking, *on the screen's side*." Clélia Zernik, *Perception-cinéma, Les enjeux stylistiques d'un dispositif* (Paris: Vrin, 2010), 52; my emphasis.

4. On the notion of "film experience," see Vivian Sobchack, *The Address of the Eye: a Phenomenology of Film Experience* (Princeton: Princeton University Press, 1992).

5. The experience of the movie spectator and its implications are the focus of Francesco Casetti's two latest books. See at least the whole chapter titled "The Place of the Observer," from his *Eye of the Century. Film, Experience, Modernity*, 141 ff., and the thematization of such an experience, which he posits in *The Lumière Galaxy: Seven Key Words for the Cinema to Come*, 4 ff.

6. On this subject, what Eisenstein writes apropos of the stereoscopic cinema is exemplary. According to him, such a cinema has "the ability to 'draw' the audience with unprecedented force into what used to be a flat surface and the ability to 'bring down' on the audience that which formerly spread over the surface of the screen." Sergei Eisenstein, "Stereoscopic Films," in *Problems of Film Direction* (Honolulu: Honolulu University Press, 2004), 81.

7. As an example: "I am one of those who, as they walk out of the movies after a cowboy film, get from the cinema hall to the bus with their legs slightly bowed, their hands at gun-reach level, staring at the yellow traffic light-pole to see where they put their horse." Marco Lombardo Radice, Lidia Ravera, *Porci con le ali* (1976) (Roma: L'Unità, 1993), 74). Of course, the memory that is sedimented in the body is what Proust names "involuntary memory," which I tried to explore precisely in this sense in my book *An Unprecedented Deformation. Marcel Proust and the Sensible Ideas*.

8. Dufrenne, *The Phenomenology of Aesthetic Experience*, 339.

9. "We may speak of the world of a subject. But what of a world of the aesthetic object? We may speak of this too—if the aesthetic object is a quasi subject, that is, if it is capable of expression" (Ibid., 196); "Because the aesthetic object is thus endowed with a sort of interiority, it is capable of expression," (Ibid., 329). The notion of "quasi-subject" returns in Dufrenne's work until his last work: see Mikel Dufrenne, *L'œil et l'oreille* (Montréal: Editions de l'Hexagone, 1987), 187.

10. More precisely, Anna Caterina Dalmasso reminds us that the notion of "quasi-subject" "retraces the Merleau-Pontian and Lacanian discovery of a 'reversed intentionality,' namely, an intentionality of the visible with respect to the gaze, which Merleau-Ponty had already seen majorly manifested in the work

of the painter." See Anna Caterina Dalmasso, "Voir selon l'écran. Autour d'une rencontre entre visibilité et théorie filmique," in Mauro Carbone, *L'empreinte du visuel: Merleau-Ponty et les images aujourd'hui* (Genève: MētisPresses, 2013), 116. Besides, what needs to be remarked is the convergency of this line of reflection and the characterization of the aura that Benjamin provides when he writes that "[t]o perceive the aura of an object we look at means to invest it with the ability to look at us in return." Walter Benjamin, «Über einige Motive bei Baudelaire» (1939–1940); trans. Harry Zohn, "On Some Motifs in Baudelaire," in Walter Benjamin, *Illuminations. Essays, and Reflections*, ed. Hannah Arendt, with a new preface by Leon Wieseltier (New York: Schocken Books, 2007), 188. Such a convergency supports the idea of an *"auraticity" of the ache-screen understood as a quasi-subject*, which we will see outlined in the present chapter.

11. See Sobchack, *The Address of the Eye*, 142.
12. Ibid.
13. Ibid.
14. Deleuze, *Cinema 2*, 280.
15. Cf. *supra*, 137, n. 91.
16. Manovich, *The Language of New Media*, 96.
17. Turkle continues by writing that the computer "does not think, yet neither it is external to thought. It is an object, ultimately a mechanism, but it behaves, interacts, and seems in a certain sense to know." Turkle, *Life on the Screen*, 22).
18. William J. T. Mitchell, *What Do Pictures Want?* (Chicago/London: The University of Chicago Press, 2005), 46; my emphasis.
19. Dufrenne, *The Phenomenology of Aesthetic Experience*, 351; there Dufrenne himself puts imagination in relation with quasi-presence.
20. Merleau-Ponty, "Eye and Mind," 126.
21. See Foucault, "The Confession of the Flesh," 195.
22. "The techno-aesthetic sentiment seems to be a category more primitive than the mere aesthetic sentiment or the technical aspect considered from the angle of the mere functionality, which is impoverishing." Simondon, "Sur la techno-esthétique" (dated 3 July 1982), in *Sur la technique (1953–1983)*, 391–92.
23. Apropos of such a domain, see the most useful article by Giovanni Carrozzini, "Esthétique et techno-esthétique chez Simondon," in *Cahiers Simondon*, no. 3, ed. Jean-Hugues Barthélémy (Paris: L'Harmattan, 2011), 51–70.
24. Simondon, *Sur la technique*, 388: "For there is, as far as each product is concerned, a margin of freedom allowing to use it for unpredicted purposes."
25. See in particular Gilbert Simondon, *Du mode de l'existence des objets techniques*, nouvelle édition revue et corrigée (Paris: Aubier, 2012), 167 ff.
26. Concerning the pictorial screen, William J. T. Mitchell claims the following: "The painting's desire, in short, is to change places with the beholder, to transfix or paralyze the beholder, *turning him or her into an image for the gaze*

of the picture in what may be called 'the Medusa effect.'" Mitchell, *What Do Pictures Want?*, 36; my emphasis.

27. Merleau-Ponty, *The Visible and the Invisible*, 147.

28. Vivian Sobchack, "The Visual and the Visible: Toward a Phenomenology of the Film Experience" [1992, 2013 (unpublished in English)]; French trans., Stefan Kristensen "Le visuel et le visible: vers une phénoménologie de l'expérience filmique," in Carbone, *L'empreinte du visuel*, 86.

29. See Jameson, *Postmodernism*, 35–36.

30. See Casetti, *The Lumière Galaxy*, 168. Casetti also highlights that this affirmation of the display is accompanied by an increasing "absence of the dark." Ibid., 205.

31. See Wajcman, *L'Œil absolu*, 11.

32. Ibid., 16.

33. Huhtamo, "Messages on the Wall," 20.

34. Ibid.

35. See *supra*, the quotation from Benjamin, 61.

36. See Deleuze, "The Brain Is the Screen: An Interview with Gilles Deleuze," 371; my emphasis.

37. Sobchack, *Carnal Thoughts*, 158.

38. Deleuze, *Difference and Repetition*, 127 ff.

39. This is one of the directions in which Žižek goes over Lacan's thought and prolongs it. Concerning this subject, see in particular Žižek, *How to Read Lacan*.

40. Ibid., 79.

41. Sobchack, *Carnal Thoughts*, 159.

42. If, on the one hand, I agree with Serge Tisseron in avoiding opposing extimacy and intimacy, on the other hand, I don't see why extimacy should necessarily be opposed to narcissism. On this subject, see in particular Serge Tisseron, "Intimité et extimité," *Communications* 88 (2011), issue directed by Antonio A. Casilli and devoted to "Cultures du numérique": 83–91.

43. On the contrary, Gilles Lipovetsky and Jean Serroy, in the "Préface à la présente édition" of *L'écran global*, insist on speaking of a "time of transparency of one's self, delivered to the wall of Facebook," for this would provide, according to them, "a live, filterless self-portrait." In order to comment on this, we have to borrow another quotation from the same page of this Preface: "The error of perspective is complete." See Gilles Lipovetsky and Jean Serroy, *L'écran global* (Paris: Seuil, 2011), XIII.

44. Dominique Cardon, "Réseaux sociaux de l'Internet," *Communications* 88 (2011): 144.

45. Ibid., 147.

46. Of course, here I refer to Christopher Lasch, *The Culture of Narcissism: American Life in an Age of Diminishing Expectations* (New York/London: W. W.

Norton, 1979), which was published in the same year as the French edition of Lyotard's *The Postmodern Condition*.

47. For a different, much more balanced and nuanced attitude concerning the same subject, see Jean-François Bach, Olivier Houdé, Pierre Léna, Serge Tisseron, *L'infant et les écrans: Un Avis de l'Académie des sciences* (Paris: Le Pommier, 2013).

Chapter 6. Making Philosophy among and through the Screens

1. Thierry Hoquet, *Cyborg philosophie: Penser contre les dualismes* (Paris: Seuil, 2011), 344. For a presentation and a discussion about the "state of the question," see in particular 343–46.

2. See Lyotard, *The Postmodern Condition*, 3.

3. See McLuhan, *Understanding Media. The Extensions of Man*. McLuhan generally affirms that "technologies are extensions of the animal organism," (235) and he considers the historical phase to which I am referring as characterized by the "technological extension of consciousness" (57).

4. As Carbone will explain in a further occurence of this expression, by *aesthetic-sensible dimension*, he means "not only perception, but also memory, imagination, and desire" (see *infra*, 100). Carbone uses the expression *aesthetic-sensible* in order to point out the difference of this peculiar aesthetic dimension (that is inaugurated and continuously renewed by one's unerasable bodily relationship with the world) from the "aesthetic-artistic" dimension. The word *aesthetic* derives from the Greek *aisthesis*, meaning *sensation*. In turn, the terms *an-aesthetization/anaesthesia/anaesthetized*, which Carbone will use later in the text (cf. *infra*, 100, 105), also refer to the same etymology [T.N.].

5. See Hidetaka Ishida, "Le temps des catastrophes dans l'âge de l'information," communication in the 5th edition of *Entretiens du Nouveau Monde industriel* organized by the "Institut de recherche et d'innovation" of the Centre Georges Pompidou, Paris 2011, unpublished transcription.

6. Richard Grusin, *Premediation: Affect and Mediality after 9/11* (London: Palgrave Macmillan, 2010).

7. Ibid., 46.

8. Ibid., 15.

9. Ishida, "Le temps des catastrophes dans l'âge de l'information," 3.

10. See Michel Foucault, "The Confession of the Flesh," in *Power / Knowledge*, 194.

11. See Montani, *Bioesthétique*, 107–109.

12. Ibid., 9.

13. Jacques Derrida declared about the attacks of 9/11: "We are talking about a trauma, and thus an event, whose temporality proceeds neither from the now that is present nor from the present that is past but from an impresentable to come [à venir] [. . .]. There is traumatism with no possible work of mourning when the evil comes from the possibility to come of the worst, from the repetition to come-though worse. Traumatism is produced by the *future*, by the *to come*, by the threat of the worst *to come*, rather than by an aggression that is 'over and done with.'" Jacques Derrida, "Autoimmunity: Real and Symbolic Suicides," in Jacques Derrida, Jürgen Habermas, *Philosophy in a Time of Terror*, presented and commented by Giovanna Borradori (Chicago/London: The University of Chicago Press, 2003), 97.

14. Ishida, "Le temps des catastrophes dans l'âge de l'information," 3; my emphasis.

15. Grusin, *Premediation*, 11; my emphasis.

16. According to Allen Feldman, the event of 9/11 has become, in turn, "a cultural prosthesis, a device for historical perception." Allen Feldman, "Ground Zero Point One" (2002), in *The World Trade Center and Global Crisis. Critical Perspectives*, ed. Bruce Kapferer (New York: Berghahn Books, 2004), 34.

17. See Claire Guillot, "Un événement photographique," *Le Monde*, 10 septembre 2011, 24.

18. Jürgen Habermas, "Fundamentalism and Terror. A Dialogue with Jürgen Habermas," in Derrida, Habermas, *Philosophy in a Time of Terror*, 28.

19. In turn, Grusin claims that "the events of 9/11 [. . .] proved less a categorical break or rupture than a kind of watershed moment, a sea change not fully evident until some time after it occurs." Richard Grusin, "Premediation," *Criticism* 46, no. 1 (Winter 2004): 21. In a slightly different way, W. J. T. Mitchell rather states that the period *following* 9/11—consisting in "the era of the War on Terror and the Bush presidency—will also be remembered as a time when the accelerated production and circulation of images in a host of new media (Facebook, YouTube, Twitter) ushered a 'pictorial turn' into public consciousness." William J. T. Mitchell, *Cloning Terror. The War of Images: 9/11 to the Present* (Chicago/London: University of Chicago Press, 2011), 2.

20. The creator of *Black Mirror*, Charlie Brooker, explained that "[t]he 'black mirror' of the title is the one you'll find on every wall, on every desk, in the palm of every hand: the cold, shiny screen of a TV, a monitor, a smartphone." Charlie Brooker, "The Dark Side of Our Gadget Addiction," *The Guardian*, December 1, 2011. https://www.theguardian.com/technology/2011/dec/01/charlie-brooker-dark-side-gadget-addiction-black-mirror; last consulted on 13 February 2018.

21. On the big data dynamics, my attention is drawn particularly by Bernard Stiegler, *La société automatique: 1. L'avenir du travail* (Paris: Fayard,

2015); trans. Daniel Ross, *Automatic Society, Vol. 1. The Future of Work* (New York: Wiley, 2016).

22. Allen Feldman, "Ground Zero Point One" (2002), in *The World Trade Center and Global Crisis. Critical Perspectives*, 30. I lingered on the implications of such a "temporal therapy" in relation to our aesthetic-sensible relation to the world and with reference to their political scope in the last chapter of my book titled *Être morts ensemble: l'événement du 11 septembre 2001*, 113 ff.

23. See Günther Anders, *Der Mann auf der Brücke. Tagebuch aus Hiroshima und Nagasaki* (München: C. H. Beck Verlag, 1959), and Michael Foessel, *Après la fin du monde, Critique de la raison apocalyptique* (Paris: Seuil, 2012).

24. Walter Benjamin, "On Some Motifs in Baudelaire," in *Illuminations. Essays and Reflections*, 159.

25. Ibid., 161.

26. Walter Benjamin, "The Work of Art in the Age of Its Technological Reproducibility," in *The Work of Art in the Age of Its Technological Reproducibility, and Other Writings on Media*, 53; my emphasis.

27. Concerning this, it has to be recalled that McLuhan uses the word *numbness* in order to describe the dynamics "that each extension brings about in the individual and society." McLuhan, *Understanding Media*, 6.

28. Edmund Husserl, *Die Krisis der europäischen Wissenschaften und die transzendentale Phänomenologie: Eine Einleitung in die phänomenologische Philosophie*, ed. Walter Biemel (The Hague: Martinus Nijhoff, 1954); trans. David Carr, *The Crisis of European Sciences and Transcendental Phenomenology* (Evanston: Northwestern University Press, 1970), 113; my emphasis.

29. Patočka, *Heretical Essays in the Philosophy of History*, 11.

30. Vivian Sobchack, "Comprehending Screens: A Meditation in Medias Res," in *Schermi/Screens*, ed. Mauro Carbone, Anna Caterina Dalmasso, *Rivista di Estetica 55* (Torino: Rosenberg and Sellier, 2014), 88.

31. See Gilbert Simondon, *L'individuation à la lumière des notions de forme et d'information* (Grenoble: Millon, 2005), 29.

32. Ibid.

33. See *supra*, 140, n. 22.

34. See Simondon, *L'individuation à la lumière des notions de forme et d'information*, 29.

35. Giorgio Agamben, "What Is an Apparatus?" in *What Is An Apparatus and Other Essays*, 14–15.

36. Simondon explains: "Because of the substantialization of the individual reality, what is generally considered as a *relation*, is in fact a dimension of individuation through which the individual becomes." Simondon, *L'individuation à la lumière des notions de forme et d'information*, 29.

37. In a completely different context, I had already dealt with such a notion, starting from the first mesmerizing paragraphs of Samuel Beckett's

Proust, in my "Preface," in Mauro Carbone, Eleonora Sparvoli (eds.), *Proust et la philosophie aujourd'hui* (Pise: ETS, 2008), 14-18. The contemporary implications of the contrast between "individuals" and "dividuals" are discussed by Arjun Appadurai in his book *Banking on Words: The Failure of Language in the Age of Derivative Finance* (Chicago: University of Chicago Press, 2015). For his part, Deleuze uses the word *dividual* in yet a different and more specific context, namely that of the analysis of film "frame" and "shot," a context from which we shall keep the following sentence: "The set cannot divide into parts without qualitatively changing each time: it is neither divisible nor indivisible, but 'dividual' [*dividuel*]." Deleuze, *Cinema 1*, 14.

38. This is what Merleau-Ponty suggests when referring to the body-mirror relation, even if he does not let its retroactive effect fully emerge: "Like all other technical objects, such as tools and signs, the mirror has sprung up along the open circuit between the seeing and the visible body. Every technique is a 'technique of the body,' illustrating and amplifying the metaphysical structure of our flesh. The mirror emerges because I am a visible seer, because there is a reflexivity of the sensible; the mirror translates and reproduces that reflexivity." Merleau-Ponty, *Eye and Mind*, 129.

39. Turkle, *Life on the Screen*, 14.

40. Ibid.; my emphasis.

41. Ibid.

42. Simondon, *L'individuation à la lumière des notions de forme et d'information*, 32.

43. Ibid., 30.

44. However, it has to be noticed that Simondon himself tends to use the notion of concept precisely when referring to the cinema: "An activity like that of the cinema is indeed capable of creating concepts whose use can be learned in the manipulation of the cinematic realities. Still, such concepts can be extended and made universal, to the point of building an actual world view." Gilbert Simondon, "Psychosociologie du cinéma" (unpublished, dated 1960), in *Sur la technique (1953–1983)*, 355.

45. "*The logic of images*—this is our thesis—is indeed a *logic of showing*." Gottfried Boehm, "Ce qui montre. De la différence iconique," in Emmanuel Alloa (ed.), *Penser l'image* (Dijon: Les presses du réel, 2010), 27. See also Gottfried Boehm, "Die Wiederkehr der Bild," in *Was ist ein Bild?* (Munich: Fink, 1994), 11–38.

Index

9/11, 53, 98, 99, 101–104, 130, 142, 143

Abrams, E., 130
acinema, 44, 46–49, 51, 126, 127–129, 134
Aelianus, 134
Aeschylus, 64, 133
Agamben, G., 72–74, 107, 108, 136, 137, 144
Alain (E.-A. Chartier), 4, 5, 8, 111
Albera, F., 113, 116, 119
Alberti, L. B., 46, 51, 58, 59, 62, 63, 66, 71, 75–77, 108, 109, 127, 131, 132, 136
Alighieri, D., 74
allegory of the cave, ix, 41, 66, 68, 75, 95
Allen, W., 81, 83, 89
Alloa, E., xi, 145
Amey, C., 134
Anders, G., 144
Andrew, D., xii, 113
apparatus, 15, 46, 50, 52, 59, 60–62, 66, 71–73, 75–77, 90, 96, 100, 101, 103, 106–109, 113, 137
Arasse, D., 63, 64, 132, 136
arche-screen, ix, 57, 66–71, 76, 81, 85, 88, 89, 135

Arendt, H., 140
Arnheim, R., 32, 121
Astre, G. A., 19
augmented reality (A.R.), 98, 101
aura, 52, 64, 132, 140
Avildsen, J., 128
Ayfre, A., 19
Azéma, M., 65, 133

Bach, J.-F., 142
Bacon, F., 123
Balthrust, O., 102
de Balzac, H., 10
Barbaras, R., xi, 120
Barthes, R., 78, 138
Barthélémy, J.-H., 140
Basterra, G., xi
Baudrillard, J., 121, 130
Bazin, A., 10, 13, 19, 21, 29, 30, 33, 38, 113, 120–122, 124, 136
Beaulieu, A., 123
de Beauvoir, S., 11
Beckett, S., 144
Belting, H., 131, 136, 138
Benjamin, A., 133
Benjamin, W., 57, 58, 60, 61, 64, 73, 76, 77, 92, 104, 105, 140, 131–133, 138, 140, 141, 144
Bennington, G., 129

Bergson, H., v, ix, x, 3–7, 9, 14–16, 18, 21–25, 34, 36, 109, 110, 111–113, 115, 133
Blanchard, T., 19
Bodini, J., xii
body, 18, 22–24, 26, 29–31, 37, 41, 44, 45, 49, 53, 59, 66, 68, 69, 93, 98, 105, 117–120, 122, 123, 127, 128, 133, 135, 137, 139, 145
Boehm, G., 145
Borradori, G., xi, 143
Bresson, R., 19, 20
Brill, A. A., 127
Broggi, P., 125
Broll, S., 131
Brooker, C., 102, 143
Brown, L., 134

Caddeo, F., xii
Carbone, M., 9, 111, 114, 116, 122, 125, 130, 132, 134, 137, 140, 141, 142, 144, 145
Cardon, D., 141
Carr, D., 144
Carrozzini, G., 140
Caruso, P., 114
Casetti, F., xi, 31, 90, 97, 121, 137, 138, 139, 141
Casey, E., 57, 58, 125, 131, 133
Cauliez, A. J., 19
Cavallin, J.-C., 138
Cézanne, P., 10, 11, 34, 36, 45, 46, 50, 114
Chaplin, C., 78
Charbonnier, L., 131, 132
Charcosset, J.-P., 16, 115
Chartier, E.-A. (Alain), 4, 5, 8, 111
Chase, M., 135
Chauvet Cave, 65, 66
chiasm, 43, 89, 125
Chiesa, L., 137
Clarac, P., 115

Cohen-Séat, G., 19
Colli, G., 136
Cometa, M., xi
Contat, M., 111, 112
Cools, A., xi
de Courville, S., xii

Dalmasso, A. C., xii, 114, 116, 119, 135, 139, 140, 144
Damas, G., 116
Davis, O., 119
De Gaetano, R., xi
Defert, D., 132
Delaunay, R., 46
Deleuze, G., x, 1, 3, 5–8, 35–38, 39, 40, 60–62, 72, 77, 84, 90, 91, 92, 111, 112, 117, 118, 122–125, 127, 132, 140, 141, 145
Delluc, L., 116
Derrida, J., 65, 106, 130, 143
Descartes, R., 21, 59, 131
de Stefanis, M., 111
desire, V, 7, 41, 43–53, 59–62, 68, 74, 76–78, 91–95, 100, 104, 132, 137, 138, 140, 142
Dias, I. M., 119
Didi-Huberman, G., 34, 64, 122, 133
Dividuation / dividuality, 105, 108
Dodd, J., 130
Doherty, B., 130
Dort, B., 130
Durafour, J.-M., 49, 126, 128, 129
Dreyfus, H. L., 114
Dreyfus, P. A., 114
Duchamp, M., 22, 47
Dufrenne, M., 83–86, 125, 139, 140
During, É., xi
Déotte, J.-L., 127, 128
Dürer, A., vii, 58, 59, 131

Eichel-Lojkine, P., 134
Eisenstein, S., 123 139

enjoyment (see also *jouissance*), 53, 92
Esquenazi, J.-P., xi
Ewald, F., 132
Ezykman, C., 134

Facebook, 94, 102, 103, 141, 143
Fahle, O., 123
Falabretti, E., xi
Fautrier, P., 9, 113
Feldman, A., 103, 104, 143, 144
Fell, J. P., 112
Ferré, A., 115
Fetveit, A., xi
figural, 24, 43
Fihman, G., 134
Fink, B., 126
Fink, H., 126
Flaxman, G., 122
Flusser, V., 136
fold / folding, 30, 68, 77, 88, 89
Foley, A. A., xi
Foss, P., 121
Foucault, M., 60, 72, 77, 85, 99, 106, 107, 132, 140, 142
frame, 49, 59, 63, 84, 89, 90, 145
Franzini, E., 114
Freud, S., 33, 45–48, 53, 69, 104, 126, 127, 128, 135
Friedberg, A., 127, 137

Galassi, J., 136
Galeta, R., 113
Gallese, V., xi
Gestalt, Gestalttheorie, Gestaltpsychologie, 11, 12, 14–16, 22–24, 27, 41, 68
Godard, J.-L., vii, 19, 20, 31, 116, 121, 124
Gordon, C., 132
Gordon, T., 131
Guillot, C., 143

Gray, H., 120, 136
Grigg, R., 126
Griffiths, J. G., 135
Grusin, R., xi, 98–101, 103–105, 142, 143
Guattari, F., 3
Gunning, T., xii
Guterman, N., 116
Guyer, P., 115, 135
Gérin, P., 10
Gödde, C., 131

Habberjam, B., 112
Habermas, J., 143
Hadot, P., 135, 137, 138
Haldane, E. S., 131
Hardy, O., 3
Harris, E., 127
Hartz, E., 113
Hegel, G. W. F., 89, 112
Heidegger, M., 112
Herzog, W., 65, 133
Hitchcock, A., 40, 73, 136, 137
Hodges, A., 111, 124, 132
Hoquet, T., 142
Houdé, O., 142
Howard, R., 132, 138
Hudek, A., 125
Huhtamo, E., 75, 91, 137, 138, 141
Hurley, R., 132
Husserl, E., 6, 7, 9, 17, 59, 99, 105, 112, 120, 125, 144

Iamblichus, 133
iconic turn, 101, 102
identity, ix, 5, 27, 38, 94, 107
individuation / individuality, 73, 77, 105–108, 127, 144
imaginary, 30, 33, 35, 44, 64, 70, 76, 123
invisible, 61, 68, 71, 91, 117
Ionescu, V., 127

Ishida, H., 98, 99, 101, 142, 143

Jacquet, F., 114
Jameson, F., 52, 53, 90, 129, 130, 141
Jaubert, M., 16, 25, 115
Jennings, M. W., 130
Jephcott, E., 130
Johansson, S., 107
Johnson, G. A., xi, 117
Joinet, J.-B., xi
Jonze, S., 107
Joughin, M., 124
jouissance, 43, 47, 48, 53, 92, 128

Kandinsky, V., 46
Kane, N., 122
Kant, I., 17, 36, 37, 69, 71, 105, 115, 116, 123, 124, 128, 135, 136
Kapferer, B., 143
Kaushik, R., xi
Keaton, B., vii, 82, 88
Kenneth, C., 115
Kenyon, A., xii
Kishik, D., 136
Klee, P., 17, 18, 29, 46, 116
Kohak, E., 130
Kondo, M., xii
Kristensen, S., 22, 24, 116, 118, 121, 141
Kuleshov, L., 12, 14–16, 137

Labrousse, R., 133
Lacan, J., 44, 45, 49, 50, 53, 94, 126, 127, 128, 130, 137, 139, 141
Lagrange, J., 132
Landes, D. A., 114
Langer, S. K., 120
Lapoujade, D., 111, 132
Larkin, E., 121
Lasch, C., 141

Laurel, S., 3
Lawrence, D. H., 122
Lefort, C., 21, 116, 117, 127
Leopardi, G., 70, 136
Lester, M., 125
Levin, T. Y., 130
Liddell, H., 134
light, 41, 42, 60, 61, 71, 72, 7–76, 90
Lindner, B., 131
Lipovetsky, G., 141
literature, 10, 11, 21, 28, 36, 51, 129, 135
Livingstone, P. N., 126
Lo Marco, L., xii
Logoz, M., 130
Lojkine, S., 134, 135
Lombardo Radice, M., 139
Lonitz, H., 131
Lopate, P., 138
Lorblanchet, M., 133
Lumière, L., 81, 137, 139, 141, 144, 145
Lydon, M., 125
Lyotard, J.-F., v, 41–53, 65, 68, 77, 91, 94, 97, 125–130, 134, 142
Léna, P., 142
L'Herbier, M., 9

make seen, 11, 41, 48
Malevitch, K., 46
Malraux, A., 114, 120
Manovich, L., 63, 132, 136, 140
Marcel, G., 19
Marey, E., 22
Marion, D., 19
Marrati, P., 113
Martin, Marcel, 19, 28, 119
Martin, Meredith, 138
Martins, J. M., xi
Massumi, B., 129
Matthews, E., 115, 135

McKeon, R., 126
McLuhan, M., 98, 100, 131, 142, 144
McQuire, S., 138
memory, 11, 34, 100, 104, 139, 142
Mepham, J., 132
Merleau-Ponty, M., v, xi, 9–17, 19–31, 33–38, 40, 42–45, 48–50, 65, 68, 69–71, 77, 83, 85, 89, 96, 109, 112–123, 125, 126, 128, 133, 135–137, 139–141
Metz, C., 18, 19, 116
Miller, J.-A., 126
Milne, P. W., 127
mirror, 44, 45, 49, 66, 77, 89, 91, 94, 126, 128, 145
Mitchell, A., 114
Mitchell, W. J. T., xi, 84, 140, 141, 143
Mitry, J., 116
mobility, 5, 6, 43, 49, 78
Moncrieff, S., 115
montage, 12, 13, 16, 31, 41, 48, 73
Montani, P., xi, 121, 122, 138, 142
Montebello, P., 117
Montinari, M., 136
Mooney, T., 113
Moran, D., 113
Mosjoukin, I., 12
Moussinac, L., 116
movement, 4–7, 10, 21–27, 29, 32–35, 38, 41, 44, 47–49, 65, 76, 98, 113, 117–119, 121, 125, 128
Musser, C., 129
mythical past, 92
mythical present, 92
mythical time, 34, 35, 53
Müller, J. M., xii

Nauckhoff, J., 136
negative screen, 68
Niederer, S., 138

Nietzsche, F., 3, 71, 130, 132, 136
Nijhuis, E., xii
Nijhuis, M., iv, xii, 9, 130
Nitsche, J., 131
Nouvelle Vague, 10, 19, 24

Olive, J.-P., 134
Olympiodorus, 134
O'Neill, J., 117
opacity, 43, 74, 76

Paci, E., 12
Panofsky, E., 59, 131
Patočka, J., 105, 130, 144
Patton, P., 111, 121, 132
Pedatella, S., 136
perception, x, 11–16, 22, 24–27, 41, 43, 45, 52, 57, 61, 63, 77, 83, 100, 104, 116, 131, 142, 143
perspective, 46, 52, 58, 59, 62, 141
phenomenology, 4, 6–11, 36, 41–44, 61, 83, 99, 100, 105, 112, 118, 125
philosophy-cinema, v, x, 79
Pickford, M., 5
Pinotti, A., xi
Plato, ix, 39, 41, 66–68, 75, 78, 95, 134
Platonism, 5, 39, 40, 95, 125
Pliny the Elder, 66, 133
Plutarch, 69, 71, 135
Porter, E. S., vii, 81, 82, 138
positive screen, 68
Pranolo, J., 121
precession, 29, 32–35, 96, 121, 123
prosthesis, 90, 92, 97–101, 103, 104, 134, 143
Proust, M., 10, 14, 17, 33–35, 37, 42, 69, 92, 115, 116, 122, 132, 145
psychology, 10, 11, 12, 13, 17, 18, 114
Pudovkin, V., 12

Pythagoras, 65, 69
Pérez-Jean, B., 134

quasi-subject, 81–86, 89, 139, 140

Ravera, L., 139
real, 32, 33, 35, 64, 81, 120, 123
reality, 6, 8, 12, 14, 15, 25, 30, 33, 49, 50, 63, 67, 83, 96, 98, 101, 111
Rembrandt (van Rijn), vii, 59, 60
Renoir, J., 129
representation, 23, 29, 42, 45, 46, 47, 49–52, 62, 72, 83, 85, 89, 103, 107, 127, 131
Rey, A., 137
Reynaert, P., xii
rhythm, 6, 12, 16, 17, 25, 28, 29
Richir, M., 59, 131, 132
Ricœur, P., 130
Risser, J., xii
Robbe-Grillet, A., 19
Rodrigo, P., xi, 13, 14, 16, 115, 126
Roffe, J., 127
Rorty, R., 131
Roth, N. A., 136
Rudrauf, D., 112
Rybalka, M., 111, 112

Sadoul, G., 24, 116, 118, 119
de Saint Aubert, E., xi, 22, 32, 117, 118, 121
Sartre, J.-P., v, 3–9, 11, 12, 27, 34–36, 55, 111–113, 115, 116, 123, 125
Schmidt, D., xii
Scott, R., 134
seduction, v, 81, 83, 86, 91, 92, 93, 138
Séglard, D., 117
sensible ideas, 34, 37, 42, 69, 125
Serroy, J., 141
Servius, 133

shadow, 41, 42, 65, 67, 68, 72, 75, 95, 134
Sheridan, A., 126
Silverman, H., 114, 125
Simondon, G., 73, 77, 85, 86, 106–109, 138, 140, 144, 145
Smith, M. B., 117
Smith, W., 123, 133
Sobchack, V., xi, 52, 53, 83, 84, 89, 92, 93, 97, 105, 125, 129, 130, 139–141, 144
Somaini, A., xi
Soper, K., 132
Soriano, M., 19
Souriau, É., 19
Sparvoli, E., 145
Stavrinaki, M., 133
Stiegler, B., xi, 65, 133, 143
Stivale, C., 125
Stockhausen, K., 102
Strachey, J., 135
Strauss, W. S., 135
Stuart Jones, H., 134

Taormina, M., 111, 124, 132
Taylor, M., 116
technology, ix, 52, 78, 97
templum, 63–66, 90, 133, 135
Teyssot, G., 136
Thomson Ross, G. R., 131
Tisseron, S., 141, 142
Todd, J.-M., 133
Tomlinson, H., 112, 113
transparency, 61, 74, 76, 125
Truffaut, F., 136, 137
truth, ix, 16, 21, 23, 41, 42, 46, 64, 65, 70–72, 75, 77, 90, 91, 96
Turarbek, L., 125
Turkle, S., 84, 108, 138–140, 145
Twitter, 103, 143

Vailland, R., 19

Vallega, A., xii
Vallega-Neu, D., xii
Valéry, P., 10
Vancheri, L., xi, 138
variations, 57, 66, 70, 71, 76, 85
Varro, 133
veil, 37, 41, 42, 46, 62, 66, 67, 71, 77, 127
Vertov, D., 12
Vigo, J., vii, 24, 26
Viola, B., 26, 119
visible, 12, 18, 30–33, 42, 43, 46, 50, 61, 65, 68, 71, 76, 77, 84, 88–91, 117, 145
vision, x, 29, 30, 32, 33, 35, 42, 43, 46, 50–52, 59, 62, 66, 68–70, 72–75, 77, 89, 90, 96, 121, 128

Wahl, J., 112
Wajcman, G., 73, 127, 131, 132, 136, 141
Wertheimer, M., 23, 118
Wieseltier, L., 140
Williams, B., 136
Williford, K., 112
Winckelmann, J. J., 4
window, 46, 48, 50–52, 57–59, 62, 63, 66, 71–77, 88–90, 108, 109, 131, 137, 139
Wood, C. S., 131
Woodward, A., 127

YouTube, vii, viii, 93, 103, 143

Zazzo, B., 19
Zazzo, R., 19
Zeno, 23
Zernik, C., 139
Zohn, H., 130, 140
Žižek, S., 40, 45, 53, 84, 92, 93, 125, 127, 130, 137, 141

www.ingramcontent.com/pod-product-compliance
Lightning Source LLC
Chambersburg PA
CBHW021144230426
43667CB00005B/247